DATE DUE

Hoover Institution Bibliographical Series: XXIII

The Treason Trial in South Africa:
A Guide to the Microfilm Record of the Trial

Thomas George Karis

The Hoover Institution
on War, Revolution, and Peace
Stanford University 1965

The Hoover Institution on War, Revolution, and Peace, founded at Stanford University in 1919 by Herbert Hoover, is a center for advanced study and research on public and international affairs in the twentieth century. The views expressed in its publications are entirely those of the authors and do not necessarily reflect the views of the Hoover Institution.

© 1965 by the Board of Trustees of
the Leland Stanford Junior University
All rights reserved
Library of Congress Catalog Card Number: 65-12624
Printed in the United States of America

PREFACE

For the historian and the political scientist, court records of political trials are like a gold mine; much worthless ore must be dug through, in hills of bulky volumes, but often there is much of value to be found. The record of the South African treason trial of 1956-1961 is a gold mine, and the aim of this guide is to provide a shaft for its exploitation.

The trial was concerned mainly with the efforts made by Africans and their allies in the four years that followed the 1952 passive resistance or "defiance" campaign. The period covered by the indictment was October 1, 1952, to December 13, 1956. But earlier events were also referred to, going back to 1912 when the African National Congress was founded. Furthermore, during the four and a quarter years in which the trial ran its course--from the arrests on December 5, 1956, to acquittal on March 29, 1961--events outside the courtroom also impinged upon it and were reflected in the record. Indeed, in the memories of many persons caught up by "the trial" either within or outside the courtroom, the trial continues vividly, even too vividly, to exist.

The legal history of the trial is so complex, the trial's dimensions are so extensive, and the level of competence often so high that the trial itself is of interest to the student of law. The record embodies probably the most thorough analysis ever made of what constitutes treason in peacetime. For the political scientist, the record is even more interesting, providing a far-reaching analysis of the nature of, and restrictions on, extraparliamentary opposition by an unenfranchised majority. The student of South African politics, in particular, will find documents and testimony regarding the policies and campaigns of protest organizations, most notably the African National Congress, and the growth of a multiracial alliance, the Congress movement.

Excessive reliance on any record of a contest of legal adversaries has pitfalls; neither the Prosecution nor the Defense seeks to elicit the whole truth. This caveat is especially necessary with regard to Communist influence. The record of the treason trial is infused with allegations regarding communism and with evidence of Communist and left-wing ideology and tactics. Communists have often been influential in South Africa, but their influence is measured largely by the extent to which they have avoided ideology and identified themselves with popular nonwhite protest or shared the burden of governmental repression. White Communists, furthermore, have played a unique role in South Africa as the only organized political group that for over thirty years (and indeed until the evolution of the Liberal Party in the late 1950's) was unqualified in its acceptance of racial equality. In emphasizing ideology, therefore, the trial's record exaggerates the importance of such matters among Africans. Any attempt to evaluate Communist influence in South Africa must go beyond the treason trial record.

The record has data on many matters: descriptions of the circumstances, conduct, and trappings of meetings; basic documents, presidential addresses, and reports of conferences and executive committees; resolutions, slogans, songs, and propaganda leaflets and flyers; newspapers, bulletins, and other periodicals; organizational and financial problems; ties between personalities and organizations within and outside South Africa and the travel of South Africans abroad; treatment in prison; and the practices of the police. A fair amount of biographical data is scattered throughout the record, which includes personal letters and memoranda. There is, finally, the prolonged testimony and cross-examination of such important African leaders as ex-Chief Albert J. Luthuli, Professor Z.K. Matthews, and Nelson Mandela. Their testimony and that of others concern the history of their own involvement in protest politics, the development of African and multiracial policies and the political thought underlying them, the practical working out of programs of action, and the role of various personalities.

A chronology of the entire trial from the first arrests to the acquittal appears below. A detailed chronology keyed to the pages of the record has been prepared only for the period from the arraignment in August 1959 to the conclusion of the evidence in October 1960. This is the period of the trial for which the Hoover Institution has a microfilm of the record.[1] The Court's judgment, the three volumes of its reasons, and the nineteen schedules accompanying these reasons are also on microfilm.[2] The phases of the trial that have not been microfilmed are the preparatory examination, the argument on the first and second indictments, and the closing arguments.

A complete set of the mimeographed record is available in the library of Northwestern University. This set includes, as far as is known, the only copy

---

[1] Pages 1-18322, reels 1-24 at the Hoover Institution.

[2] These are all on reel 25 at the Hoover Institution.

PREFACE   v

(outside of official holdings) of the record from August 1, 1958, to April 20, 1959, the period of argument on the two indictments. Northwestern University, Boston University, and the University of California at Los Angeles also have a copy of the microfilm held by the Hoover Institution. The library of the South African Institute of Race Relations in Johannesburg has a complete set of the record of the preparatory examination and an almost complete set of the record of the trial for the period from the arraignment to the conclusion. A complete set of the record covering this latter period is in the library of the University of South Africa in Pretoria. There are also at least partial sets held privately, and there is, of course, the complete set held in the Pretoria Supreme Court.

The record would be even more voluminous than it is if it included the full text of all the exhibits in the trial. Thousands of documents used in the preparatory examination were not introduced later in the trial proper, and many others were not used during the trial under the second and last indictment.

The 4,000 to 5,000 documents submitted as evidence by the Prosecution included printed books and pamphlets, magazines and newspapers, mimeographed reports, bulletins and circulars, typewritten and handwritten documents, and a miscellaneous assortment of flyers, memoranda, and official and personal letters. These were found in offices and homes and at meetings, on open tables, in bookcases, in desks and briefcases, and in the possession of individuals during more than a thousand searches and raids. For the most part, the record includes only the portions of documents that were read in court. Some documents that were read in part were later inserted into the record in full without being read. Some documents appear in the record only by their title or by a brief description. Others were referred to on many occasions in order to indicate that they had been in the possession of one of the accused.

Photostats of a large proportion of the documents themselves and a few originals are in the library of the Institute of Race Relations. The Hoover Institution deposited a microfilm of this collection with the Cooperative African Microfilm Project (CAMP) at the Mid-West Inter-Library Center.[3] In addition, Northwestern University possesses a large collection of original documents pertaining to the trial.

For the student who goes to the record, the most useful sections of this guide are the chronologies, the chart and list of names of the accused and alleged co-

---

[3] While this book was in press, the name was changed from Mid-West Inter-Library Center to Center for Research Libraries.

conspirators, and the indexes. In order to add to the general usefulness of this booklet, the full or abridged text of selected documents of the Prosecution and the Defense and also the judgment of the Court (excluding its lengthy reasons) have been included, although these may not strictly belong in a guide.

I wish to thank Dr. Peter Duignan, Curator of the Africa Collection of the Hoover Institution, for his advice and patience; Miss Evelyn Love, for her general assistance; Miss Toni Middleton for the preparation of the indexes; and Professor Gwendolen Carter for reviewing the final manuscript. I am also indebted to friends in South Africa who have reviewed it but do not wish to be named. I alone, of course, am to blame for errors.

Thomas Karis

White Plains, New York
July 1964

CONTENTS

	Page
PREFACE	iii
I. THE TRIAL AND ITS POLITICAL MEANING	1
Before the Arrests	2
During the Trial	9
The Course of the Trial	12
The Prosecution	17
The Defense	20
The Judgment	22
Results and Reactions	24
The Trial's Aftermath	27
II. CHRONOLOGICAL GUIDE	32
Chronology	32
Guide to the Microfilm Record	35
III. THE ACCUSED AND ALLEGED CO-CONSPIRATORS	46
Chart Showing Main Changes	46
List of Names	47
IV. SELECTED DOCUMENTS	51
The Second Indictment	51
The Prosecution's Opening Address	55
The Prosecution's Summary of Facts	58
Preliminary Statement by the Defense	64
Admissions Made by the Defense	64
Judgment of the Special Criminal Court	67
V. INDEXES	77
Numbering of Pages by Date, Volume, and Reel	77
List of Selected Documents	86
List of Selected Transcripts of Meetings	90
Index of Documents by Organization or Person	94
Index of Names	101
BIBLIOGRAPHY	122

I. THE TRIAL AND ITS POLITICAL MEANING*

The judgment in the great South African treason trial of December 1956 – March 1961 affirmed the nonviolent intentions during the indictment period of the African National Congress (ANC), the historic organ of extraparliamentary protest for the unenfranchised African majority. The trial itself occurred, however, in the last stage of the period of nonviolence. Its duration overlapped the shooting at Sharpeville on March 21, 1960, the five-month national emergency that followed, and the official ban on both African nationalist movements, the ANC and the newer Pan-Africanist Congress (PAC). Until it was driven underground, the ANC officially maintained its policy of nonviolence, although even before this event some important individuals within the movement may have abandoned their hope for peaceful change. At any rate, the period since the trial's conclusion is one in which both sides--the official forces of white supremacy and most of those African leaders who are in exile or underground--accept violence as unavoidable.

The early-morning arrests made on December 5, 1956, and some days later were aimed at most of the leaders of the extraparliamentary opposition to South Africa's racial policies. One hundred fifty-six persons were accused of being members of "a country-wide conspiracy" inspired by international communism to overthrow the State by violence. The most important organization represented by the accused was the ANC, whose leading officials were arrested. Others belonged to organizations allied with it in the so-called Congress Alliance or Liberatory Movement. The trial that followed was described by Gerald Gardiner, an early British observer, as "unique in legal history...unique in the number of the accused, in the weight of the documents, in the length of the proceedings and, not least, in the extraordinary width of the laws applicable."[1] Later, L.J. Blom-Cooper observed,

---

*This essay draws heavily on two of the author's earlier publications: (1) The article "The South African Treason Trial" in <u>Political Science Quarterly</u>. Reprinted with permission from Political Science Quarterly, Volume 76, No. 2, June 1961, pp. 217-240. (2) The section "South Africa" in Gwendolen M. Carter, ed., <u>Five African States</u>, pp. 480-482, 489-492, 606-607. Copyright 1963 by Cornell University. Used by permission of Cornell University Press.

[1] "The South African Treason Trial," <u>Journal of the International Commission of Jurists</u>, 1 (Autumn 1957): 43, 58.

"Not since the burning of the Reichstag in Berlin in 1933--with the notable exception of the special trials at Nuremberg--has a trial attracted such international attention."[2] Yet the trial presented no special problem regarding legal correctness or, except during the emergency that followed Sharpeville, judicial impartiality. Some substantive questions concerning the meaning of treason in South African law were involved in it. But what made the trial particularly interesting and important was its political meaning, that is, the question of its effect on prospects for racial reconciliation in South Africa.

Before the historical background of the trial is given, a brief statement should be made regarding the South African law of high treason. This law is not precise, nor were its precedents directly applicable to the case since they had arisen in circumstances of war or rebellion. The law of treason derives from Roman-Dutch common law, which is vaguer and less restrictive than English statutory definitions or the even more rigid definition in the United States constitution: "Treason against the United States shall consist only in levying war against them, or in adhering to their enemies, giving them aid and comfort." "High Treason" in South Africa, according to the standard treatise on criminal law, "is committed by those who with a hostile intention disturb, impair or endanger the independence or safety of the State, or attempt or actively prepare to do so."[3] As in England and the United States, it is punishable by death.

Before the Arrests

The background of the efforts that led to the treason trial stretches far back in South African history. African aspirations were encouraged in the nineteenth century by the Cape Colony's liberal tradition, which was largely transplanted from the outside. In 1853 the franchise for elections to the newly established Cape Parliament was made nonracial, with literacy and economic qualifications lower than the level desired by the white representatives of the colonists. "Bantu political liberalism" sought expression in the 1880's, and the Cape Parliament, by that time largely autonomous in domestic matters, began the process of curbing the political expansion of the Bantu electorate. By raising franchise qualifications, the

---

[2] "The South African Treason Trial: R. v. Adams and Others," *International and Comparative Law Quarterly*, 8 (January 1959): 59.

[3] F.G. Gardiner and C.W.H. Lansdown, *South African Criminal Law and Procedure* (Cape Town, 1957), II, 987.

Cape Parliament avoided the imposition of a political color bar.

Political parties were fairly evenly matched from 1896 to 1910, and the African voter held the balance of power in seven Cape constituencies. His vote, for which white candidates asked, was instrumental in preventing the adoption of discriminatory legislation that was being adopted elsewhere in southern Africa. But his influence was to be diminished steadily.

The Act of Union of 1910 marked a further stage in the decline of liberalism. The defeated Boer ex-republics had retained their exclusive white franchise and, at the national convention, their representatives considered any change intolerable. Nor would they tolerate the presence of nonwhites in the Union Parliament, although nonwhites had been eligible for election (none had been elected, however) to the Cape Parliament. The franchise issue was resolved by leaving the matter to each province, and the Cape franchise was entrenched by requiring a special amendment procedure. But membership in the Union Parliament was restricted to whites.

Of the racially discriminatory legislation enacted in the following two decades, the Natives Land Act of 1913 was a source of exceptional grievance to Africans. It prohibited the acquisition of land except in the reserves. Moreover, continuing efforts were made to eliminate the African franchise. The number of Africans on the common roll had reached 16,481 in 1929; in 1935, it was down to 10,628. In 1936, over the outspoken opposition of African political organizations and white liberals, the newly fused United Party under Generals Hertzog and Smuts enacted a bill that had been pending in various forms for nearly a decade. With only eleven members of the two houses of Parliament voting in opposition, African voters were removed to a separate or communal roll for the election of three white representatives to the House of Assembly. The so-called Hertzog settlement also provided for the indirect election of four white Senators by Africans throughout the country and for the purchase of land to enlarge the reserve areas.

Until 1936, many African leaders continued to hope that cooperation with liberally inclined whites would bring about a reduction in racial discrimination and a progressive sharing of political power. The organ that continually expressed African aspirations following the formation of the Union was the African National Congress. In order to protest violations of the liberal tradition and to promote a sense of national identity among Africans, members of a small class of educated and conservative Africans had organized the ANC (originally the South African Native National Congress) in 1912 in cooperation with tribal chiefs. Agitation flared occasionally after World War I, beginning with a demonstration in 1919 against the carrying of passes. The first conference of African, Colored, and Indian organizations was held in 1927, but no common front was formed. In 1930-1931 attempts, inspired by Communists, were made to organize pass-burning demonstrations and boycotts of beer halls. Nevertheless, with some notable exceptions, leadership remained through the 1930's in the hands of professional men and church leaders whose nationalism was coupled with respect for tribal authority.

Meanwhile, the South African Communist Party, fully accepting African equality, had been formed by whites in 1921. The party recruited and trained some able Africans but was weakened by its adherence to directions from Moscow and made little headway among African intellectuals.

The loosely organized Industrial and Commercial Workers' Union, on the other hand, overshadowed the ANC during the late 1920's. Its flamboyant leadership and practical policies attracted many thousands of followers. But after squabbles over the leadership, major financial difficulties, and internal divisions including the ousting of Communists, the ICU disintegrated.

The year 1936 marked a low point in the process of African disillusionment with the promise of liberalism. The hopes of some African leaders for effective consultation, if not participation, were temporarily sustained by the establishment in that year of an advisory Natives' Representative Council. But the Council was unable during the following decade to evolve into an effective body and thus to win the support of Africans, including its own members. Its virtual demise came in 1946, when it suspended its sittings because of the absence of consultation and in protest against the violence with which the United Party government, led by General Smuts, had broken a strike of African mineworkers.

From 1936 to 1949, a new urban generation of Africans came of age. Dr. A. B. Xuma, an American-educated physician, who was president of the ANC from 1940 to 1949, concentrated on building an economically well-established urban movement that could act independently of whites and Indians. The wartime idealism of the Atlantic Charter was given African expression in a 1945 statement of "African Claims," which called for "the abandonment of any policy and all practices that discriminate against the African in any way whatsoever." The omnibus nature of the ANC was indicated by the cooperation of both conservative anti-Communists and Moses Kotane, the secretary-general of the South African Communist Party, in the formulation of "African Claims." These claims were pressed in further manifestoes, in boycotts, and in strikes. White, Indian, and African radicals organized multiracial demonstrations, and nonwhite trade unions claimed 50,000 members. Greater militancy culminated in 1946 in the African mineworkers' strike, noted above. In the same year, Dr. Xuma himself joined with Indian leaders to protest against discriminatory legislation aimed at Indians.

In 1949 the ANC Youth League, which had been organized during the war and sought more militant action, brought about Dr. Xuma's displacement and the adoption of a "Programme of Action." This document called for an end to cooperation with governmental institutions and for boycotts, strikes, and civil disobedience. The main inspiration of the Youth League was militant African nationalism, not communism. Indeed, some leaders of the Youth League, for example, Nelson Mandela, considered membership in the Communist Party incompatible with membership in the Youth League.

During 1949-1952, the ANC moved toward closer multiracial cooperation. The new Nationalist government's racial legislation affected all nonwhites and widened the common ground upon which could be built a combined opposition of Africans, Coloreds, Indians, and allied whites. The Suppression of Communism Act of 1950, in particular, defined communism so loosely and broadly that it appeared as a common threat to all extraparliamentary opponents of the government. Thus it strengthened the tendency of the younger ANC leaders, including Mandela, to cooperate more closely with Communists of all races. (The Communist Party, which dissolved itself just before being banned, had approximately 2,500 members. Nearly half of them were Africans, but the most influential members were whites and Indians.) Leaders of the Transvaal ANC and the South African Indian Congress cooperated in sponsoring a one-day strike on May Day in 1950, which led to the killing by the police of eighteen persons and the wounding of thirty. The deaths were commemorated on June 26, which has become a sacred day in the calendar of protest. Joint planning for mass action continued, and on June 26, 1952, the defiance campaign of passive resistance to "unjust laws" began.

By deliberately violating restrictions on African movements and minor apartheid regulations, the demonstrators sought to protest against four new Nationalist laws in addition to the older pass laws and (as a protest against lack of land) measures aimed at culling cattle to reduce overgrazing. The four laws were those designed to confine each racial group to its own "group area," to re-establish tribal authority, to remove Coloreds from the common roll, and to suppress "communism." The ANC's membership of around 15,000 to 20,000 grew to 100,000; and about 8,500 volunteers, mostly Africans but including Indians and Coloreds, went to jail.

While the campaign was still in progress, rioting and violence occurred in three cities in response to police arbitrariness, and some three dozen nonwhites and several whites were killed. The period covered by the trial's indictment began on October 1, 1952, that is, a few days before the first riots. However, the Prosecution during the trial did not allege any direct connection between the ANC and the riots. According to Gwendolen Carter, the riots "were neither stimulated nor condoned by the African National Congress."[4]

The next period, 1953-1956, began with the enactment of punitive legislation that seriously increased the penalties, including whipping, for advocacy of, as well as participation in, any future campaign of protest; the period ended with the treason arrests. The challenge to authority became less direct as tactics shifted from disobedience to demonstration, but a climax was reached with the formation of a multiracial front. On June 25-26, 1955, the ANC, the South African Indian Congress, the newly organized Congress of Democrats (a few hundred whites, including some members of the banned Communist Party), and the South African Colored People's Organization joined in holding a so-called Congress of the People at Kliptown outside Johannesburg. The latter two organizations supplied the white and Colored spokes of the four-spoke wheel that symbolized the Congress of the People. Other organizations allied to the Congress movement and figuring in the treason arrests had been formed during the two years preceding June 1955: the South African Peace Council, the South African Indian Youth Congress, the Federation of South African Women, and the South African Congress of Trade Unions.

Nearly 3,000 delegates to the Congress of the People endorsed a Freedom Charter, which was to be the key document in the Prosecution's case. The Charter was largely free of Communist phraseology although it displayed traces of Communist style. In the main, it rang the changes on one theme: all racial discrimination must be abolished and equal rights must be guaranteed for all. This theme had constantly recurred at least since 1943, when the new ANC constitution had proclaimed as an aim "the freedom of the African people from all discriminatory laws whatsoever." The Charter asserted that "our people have been robbed of their birthright" but attempted no historical explanation of the status quo, suggested no philosophy of social change, and proposed no program of action. Except for a few generalities, the Charter ignored international affairs. "These freedoms we will fight for," it concluded, "side by side, throughout our lives, until we have won our

---

[4] The Politics of Inequality (New York, 1958), p. 374.

liberty." "Freedom in Our Lifetime" appeared on banners at the rally but not in the Charter itself. Some delegates were reported to have said "freedom in the lifetime of Luthuli," the president general, who was about fifty-seven and had had a heart attack.

The Charter was not officially adopted by the ANC until early in 1956, and then only over considerable opposition. The particular importance of the Charter in the history of the ANC's demands is that public ownership of mineral wealth, banks, and monopoly industry and a redivision of the land among those who worked it were mentioned for the first time. Otherwise, the Charter envisioned a social welfare state in which industry and trade were "controlled" for the public welfare, workers were free to form trade unions and to make wage agreements with employers, "no one shall go hungry," and "rest, leisure, and recreation shall be the right of all."

Leading Communists of all races deserve special credit for the skillful preparation and staging of the Congress of the People, but their ideological influence was limited. The Charter itself was clearly not a Communist document. Nor did the Communists, who had worked closely with Africans inspired by nationalism and Indians inspired by Gandhi, control either the omnibus ANC or the Indian Congress. Ex-Chief Albert Luthuli, a liberal who was president of the ANC from 1952 on, accepted support from all quarters in working for equality. Luthuli has insisted that he will accept the cooperation of Communists only so long as they are not in control.

African leaders continued to be divided by the persistent question of whether or not to collaborate with radical whites, Coloreds, and Indians, whom anti-Communist leaders like Dr. Xuma especially distrusted. Nevertheless, nearly all African leaders were in basic agreement on the unacceptability of a white policy that promised to move neither towards political integration nor towards fully independent African states in the foreseeable future. Late in 1956, both Xuma and Luthuli took part in the most widely representative African conference to be held since 1935 and 1936. The conference, called by a federation of African Christian ministers, found virtually no hope for racial harmony in officially sponsored proposals for separate development and appealed for further discussion with whites.

During the period after the defiance campaign, protest meetings and publications were not generally forbidden, but administrative restrictions on the movements of nonwhite and radical opponents became increasingly severe. Police surveillance and raids amounted to harassment and intimidation. The police attended meetings and conducted numerous raids, taking notes and collecting evidence that was to be grist for the Prosecution in the forthcoming trial. There were a thousand of these raids in the months following the June 1955 meeting. "Everything still has to be correlated," the Minister of Justice told Parliament in April 1956, "but it is expected that about two hundred people will be charged" with treason and other offenses. Presumably the arrests occurred only when at last everything had been "correlated"--at least to the satisfaction of the Special Branch.

The 156 persons arrested were a racially mixed and ideologically diverse group. Two-thirds, or 104, were Africans. They ranged from Moses Kotane, who had been secretary-general of the Communist Party, to Luthuli, a Christian and liberal who has described his outlook as having much in common with that of the British Labor Party, and to some Africanists who became members of the PAC when it was formed in 1959. Few of the Africans had been members of the Communist Party. The older and younger generations were represented notably by Professor Z.K. Matthews, academically the most distinguished African in South Africa, and his son Joe, a brilliant left-wing leader. Dr. Xuma himself was included as an alleged co-conspirator in the first, but not the second, indictment. Many minor African politicians were arrested or listed later among the alleged co-conspirators, including one African politically emasculated by Moral Re-Armament.

Forty-four of the persons arrested were whites and Indians (nearly the same number of each), and eight were Coloreds. Most of the whites and some of the Indians had been members of the Communist Party or had an outlook indistinguishable from those who had been party members. The outlook of the others ranged across a wide spectrum, from persons attracted by the Communist world peace movement to persons who identified themselves with the humanitarian cause of African advancement. Some of the Indians were followers of Gandhi.

On the other hand, some leading Communists who had long been under ban and against whom there was little evidence of activity during the indictment period were not arrested. Dr. Yusuf Dadoo, for example, a professed Communist who was highly respected as a trustworthy ally by many non-Communist Indians and was president of the South African Indian Congress, was not arrested or even included in the lists of alleged co-conspirators. Some Communists among the accused were later dismissed or transferred to the list of co-conspirators.

About a year after the arrests, Luthuli and Oliver Tambo, the ANC's second-ranking official at the time, were among sixty-one accused who were dismissed. Their dismissal seemed (and still seems) inexplicable when it later became clear that the alleged violent policy of the ANC itself was the central issue of the trial.

During the Trial

During three months early in 1957, the successful boycott of Johannesburg buses by more than 50,000 Africans demonstrated the readiness of Africans who share an economic grievance to cooperate effectively and almost spontaneously in local protest. The boycott was settled only after contact, through intermediaries, between white businessmen and ANC leaders among the accused.

Meanwhile, younger and, in some cases, less disciplined African leaders were urging greater militancy, racial assertiveness and self-reliance, and identification with Pan-Africanism. Immediately prior to the general election of April 1958, the ANC and its Congress allies sponsored a three-day stay-at-home demonstration. Because of confused leadership, African dissension, and effective countermeasures by the government, the demonstration was a fiasco. A year later, African nationalists who opposed the Congress Alliance and were outspokenly anti-Communist broke away from the ANC and formally established the Pan-Africanist Congress.

Following the election, progovernment Afrikaner intellectuals began holding a series of private meetings with Africans, including ANC leaders on trial for treason and PAC leaders. Similar meetings, which included big-business men, were held beginning in 1959 by members of Parliament who had resigned from the United Party and joined the new Progressive Party. Although their premises varied widely, these whites based their hope for eventual African consent on the preliminary step of African consultation.

On March 21, 1960, at Sharpeville, south of Johannesburg, the police killed 72 Africans and wounded about 186 in a crowd that was demonstrating its support for a new defiance campaign against the carrying of passes and, according to the police, was threatening to overrun them. The campaign that occasioned these and later disturbances was initiated by the PAC and opposed by the ANC on the ground that it was "sensational" and might not succeed. After the shooting, however, Luthuli called for a stay-at-home Day of Mourning and made the defiant gesture of burning his pass.

The government, seeking a showdown, exercised for the first time the power granted to it by legislation enacted after the passive resistance campaign of 1952. It proclaimed an emergency, thus freeing itself from the restrictions of habeas corpus. By enacting legislation that resulted in the outlawing of both the ANC and the PAC, the government took one of the major actions that probably would have followed a successful prosecution of the trial. By arresting and indefinitely detaining 1,900 persons seized in early-morning raids, it cracked down on political suspects whose names were apparently on a standing list, including pre-1950 members of the Communist Party who had not been arrested in December 1956. (More than 17,000 African "idlers" were also detained.) By jailing leaders of the anti-Communist Liberal Party without explanation and for the first time, the government acted in a manner predicted by critics who had seen danger to all opponents of official policy in the breadth of the Prosecution's treason trial argument. By convicting the PAC leaders during the first six weeks after Sharpeville for incitement and by imposing penalties ranging from whipping to three years in jail, the government demonstrated again its ability to act effectively in cutting down African leadership.

The trial took on a new importance. The government, maintaining that a Communist-inspired conspiracy was behind the Sharpeville demonstrations, looked upon the trial as a partial substitute for the judicial inquiry unsuccessfully demanded by the parliamentary opposition. No major commission of inquiry would be appointed before the trial was concluded, the Prime Minister said on May 20, 1960, the last day of Parliament, "as this trial itself has in part the character of an inquiry into the causes of disturbances." Earlier, in explanation of the "reign of terror which threatens public safety," the Minister of Justice quoted from Robert Resha's "murder! murder!" speech (noted below) and other evidence for the Prosecution, although he added, "I shall...suppress the names of the speakers, in view of the fact that there is a case pending."

After the emergency ended on August 31, 1960, the surface of South Africa's life resumed the appearance of normality, including the resumption of extraparliamentary activity by the ANC's allied organizations in the Congress movement. The left-wing and pro-Congress weekly New Age resumed publication. Many persons who had been detained became publicly active again, among them ANC and PAC members who were not themselves banned.

Leading whites, including supporters of the government and representatives of commerce and industry, made the most urgent appeals in 1960 for "consultation" with Africans that were ever heard in South Africa. In reply to suggestions that ANC and PAC leaders should be among these Africans, the Minister of Justice said that these organizations had a combined membership of "only about 70,000" and constituted "a small coterie of terrorists" who want "our country." The ban on both organizations was renewed in 1961 and annually thereafter.

THE TRIAL AND ITS POLITICAL MEANING 11

Meanwhile, Africans made a last effort to organize a mass public rally, the All-In African Conference at Pietermaritzburg, Natal, on March 25-26, 1961. The conference took place just three days before the sudden ending of the treason trial. The origin of the conference lay in an invitation extended by Luthuli, who was restricted to his home district in Natal, Professor Z.K. Matthews, and three others to a widely representative group of about forty African men and women. The group met in a Consultative Conference on December 16-17, 1960, and agreed on the need for "effective use of non-violent pressures against apartheid" and the calling of a national convention representing all South Africans. Genuine hope existed that at least a multiracial conference could be held as the culmination of the series of private discussions that had been taking place, especially since the general election of 1958, between whites and nonwhites, including Luthuli and others involved in the trial.

A continuation committee was set up whose members represented an extraordinarily wide spectrum of African opinion. However, the united front embodied in the committee was destroyed and the PAC and Liberal members withdrew as a result of suspicions that former ANC members, guided by "the invisible hand" (in the words of an African leader of the Liberal Party) of Communists in the background, were distorting the mandate for unity and imparting to the future conference an ideological slant that served Communist ends.

With former ANC members predominant in the planning, the All-In Conference met in March 1961, with more than a thousand Africans from many parts of the country in attendance. They observed the dramatic appearance of, and heard a keynote address by, Nelson Mandela. Mandela was one of the founders of the ANC Youth League and former president of the ANC in the Transvaal. He was able for the first time in nine years to attend a meeting since the government had overlooked the expiration of his ban and had not renewed it. The conference issued an ultimatum to the government for the calling of a national convention before May 31, 1961, the day the Republic was to be proclaimed. Assuming that the ultimatum would be ignored, the conference urged Africans to prepare for a three-day stay-at-home demonstration at that time.

[Postscript: Since the All-In Conference and the coincidental ending of the treason trial, no segment of the African opposition has attempted--or in the foreseeable future will attempt--a mass public rally for the announcement of widespread demonstrations to be held many weeks later. Mandela's statements describing the planned stay-at-home demonstration of May 29-31, 1961, and the distribution of thousands of leaflets had the familiar appearance of similar tactics in the past. But Mandela's disappearance underground and the secrecy of the planning reflected the new precariousness of nonwhite protest. The stay-at-home, which was openly opposed by members of the PAC, failed to mobilize mass support but succeeded in triggering a large-scale mobilization of police and military forces. The mobilization revealed the extent of white insecurity and dampened the festivities that accompanied the proclamation of the Republic. With the coming of the Republic, the banned ANC entered a new period in which its leaders began publicly to accept violence as unavoidable.]

The Course of the Trial

The course of the trial appeared bewilderingly complex because of the great bulk of the evidence, the seemingly endless series of further particulars and amendments to the indictment, the discharge without explanation of two-fifths of the accused, the split of the remaining accused into separate groups, the Court's dismissal of a new indictment against one group, and anomalies in the inclusion of some persons and exclusion of others among those arrested, discharged, or regrouped. On August 5, 1959, after describing the fairness of the proceedings as the trial's "one bright spot," the Times of London observed that "for the rest, darkness and confusion prevail."

Much of the delay and procedural complexity can be explained by the circumstances of an unprecedented mass trial in a legal system whose procedure was based mainly on English common law. The anomalies and permutations in the lists of the accused and co-conspirators can partly be explained by legal considerations of evidence and joinder and the practical difficulties of handling a large number of defendants. Ignorance about the leaders of the extraparliamentary opposition is another explanation offered by critics, who direct their criticism on this score at the Attorney-General of the Transvaal. The legal issues were clear, although poorly illuminated by precedent, and became narrower as the trial progressed. The trial had seven phases:

Phase I. Preparatory Examination. December 1956 - January 1958.

The preparatory inquiry occupied some nine months in Johannesburg and was concluded when the presiding magistrate found "sufficient reason for putting the accused on trial on the main charge of high treason." Meanwhile, despite the gravity of the charge, the accused were released in December 1956, on bail that was nominal: £250 for whites, £100 for Indians and Coloreds, and £50 for Africans. In December 1957, furthermore, the Attorney-General announced that he was withdrawing charges against sixty-one of the accused, including Luthuli.

Phase II. The First Indictment Argued. August-October 1958.

A three-judge special criminal court in Pretoria heard legal argument on the adequacy of the indictment. Proceedings were temporarily suspended when the Prosecution withdrew the indictment, an occurrence described by one observer as unparalleled in English legal history.[5]

Before the indictment was withdrawn, its scope had been narrowed. Originally it had charged that the accused were guilty of high treason because they had conspired and acted "in concert and with common purpose" to overthrow the State by violence. The indictment also had included two alternative charges of contravening the Suppression of Communism Act. (These charges were concerned with the furtherance of "communism" rather than, as in high treason, acting with hostile intent to subvert the State.) The Court quashed one of the two alternative charges and ordered the Prosecution to supply additional particulars regarding the other. The Court also ordered the Prosecution to tell each accused how he was affected by the difference between allegations of "conspiracy" and allegations of "concert and common purpose." The Prosecution's response was to drop the remaining charge under the Suppression of Communism Act, leaving only the main charge of high treason, and to delete the words "acting in concert and with common purpose," leaving only the allegation of conspiracy. Both the Court and the Defense still assumed that, if conspiracy was not proved, the Prosecution would attempt to establish the guilt of each accused for separate overt acts of high treason. But on September 29 the leader of the Prosecution announced that he was relying on adherence to "conspiracy pure and simple." "If the Crown fails to prove conspiracy," he said, "then all the accused go free."

During argument, the Court appeared to side with the Defense in its view that the planning of violence was necessary for treason and that the Prosecution should supply particulars of the facts upon which it relied in its inference that the

---

[5] Bail conditions came to an end. From that time on, except while detained during the emergency in 1960, the accused were free. Their obligation to attend Court was in response to a summons to do so. After the emergency, the Prosecution applied to the Court to order the rearrest of the accused. The Court held it had no power to do so since the bail had lapsed.

accused intended to act violently. The Prosecution, on the other hand, accused the Defense and indirectly the Court of failing to cooperate in "streamlining" the indictment. The Prosecution may have avoided a quashing of the indictment by withdrawing it.

Phase III. The Second Indictment Argued. January-June 1959.

The trial was resumed in a more manageable form under a second indictment against only thirty defendants. Under the new indictment, the issues of the trial were narrowed still further. The Prosecution's case was now, and for the remainder of the trial, limited to proving the intention of the accused to act violently. The crux, according to the particulars, was narrower yet: whether or not violence was the policy of the ANC and its allied organizations, to which the thirty accused belonged. Therefore, although the thirty accused were distinguished by the more violent tone of their rhetoric, Luthuli and other ANC leaders who testified for the Defense were, in effect, as much on trial as were the thirty.

Of the ninety-one accused, fifteen had been members of the Communist Party and thirty were whites or Indians, but only two of the Communists and five of the whites and Indians were included among the final thirty accused. Only a few of the African accused were ANC leaders of importance. The alleged adherence of the thirty to the conspiracy covered a shorter period of time than that covered by the original indictment (instead of October 1, 1952, the period began on February 1, 1954, running until December 13, 1956), but the Prosecution's evidence against the thirty covered the longer period and included speeches and documents of the persons originally accused and the co-conspirators. No particular conspiracy by the thirty was alleged.

After argument on the adequacy of the indictment was concluded, the Court refused on March 2 to dismiss the indictment and ordered the Prosecution to supply particulars, which became known colloquially as the "violence particulars." The Defense had questioned the nature of overt acts on which the Prosecution could rely in showing hostile intent. If the overt acts were spoken or written words, the Defense argued, such words in the absence of an external enemy should at the very least amount to an incitement to violence or sedition. Following the test of intent and tendency, though referring also to circumstances, the Court disagreed, "provided the words, in the circumstances, manifest the hostile intent and provided they tend toward the accomplishment of the criminal design."

The ruling was referred to the Appellate Division of the Supreme Court, and the trial was postponed. Such an appeal at this stage had no precedent in South African (and probably none in British) legal history. In mid-June the Appellate Division ruled that it had no jurisdiction on questions of law arising from an unconcluded trial.

Meanwhile, an event occurred that was an aberration from the normal course of events, although it was hailed by the trial's critics at home and abroad as a victory. The official announcement in November 1958 that the trial would proceed against only thirty of the accused had stated that the remaining sixty-one would also be reindicted on a charge of treason and that their trial would begin on April 20, 1959, or afterwards. Presumably they were to be tried after the conclusion of the trial of the thirty. But on April 20, no later date having been set, the sixty-one appeared in court. They had been divided into two groups, each facing an indictment (covering different periods of time) that was essentially the same as that faced by the thirty in January but totally lacking in particularity. Because of this failure, the Court quickly and surprisingly granted the Defense motion to dismiss the indictment. The sixty-one still faced reindictment.

Speaking later, on May 12, 1959, about "the ordinary course of justice," the Minister of Justice said: "This trial will be proceeded with, no matter how many millions of pounds it costs.... What does it matter how long it takes?"

Phase IV. The Trial Begins: Arraignment and Evidence.
August 1959 - March 1960.

Two years and eight months after their arrest, the thirty accused were at last arraigned. Each pleaded not guilty. For over two months, some 150 witnesses for the Prosecution testified about more than 4,000 documents, and for nearly six weeks the witness stand was occupied by Andrew Murray, professor of philosophy at the University of Cape Town, the Prosecution's expert witness on communism. The Prosecution concluded on March 10. The Defense called its first witness a few days later and began the examination of Luthuli on March 21.

Phase V. The Trial during the State of Emergency. March - July 1960.

The trial entered a new phase after the shooting at Sharpeville on March 21, the declaration of a national emergency, and the outlawing of the ANC. The accused, except one who absconded, were among some 1,900 political suspects arrested in early-morning raids. (Tambo, the ANC's second-ranking official, escaped from the country.) The Court adjourned. When it met again late in April, the Defense counsel withdrew at the request of the accused after the Court had overruled protests that witnesses would be imperiled if they testified during the emergency. "We do not believe," said Duma Nokwe, an African of left-wing sympathies among the accused and the first African to become an advocate in the Transvaal, "that a political trial can be properly conducted under conditions amounting virtually to martial law."

Nokwe and others among the accused continued to examine witnesses. The accused marked time by examining one white, one Indian, and one Colored witness regarding conditions in South Africa and avoiding testimony on the ANC's policy. Many questions were asked by Mr. Justice Rumpff, the presiding judge. With the easing of emergency conditions and at the request of the accused, one of the Defense counsel returned on July 18.

Phase VI. The Defense Back to Normal: Evidence Concluded.
August - October 1960.

Nearly all the Defense counsel returned on August 1. Later in the month, the Defense for the first time challenged the impartiality of one of the judges, Mr. Justice Rumpff, on the ground that the cumulative effect of his interventions gave the impression of unfairness. The judge rejected the challenge, and the Court gave permission to appeal if the verdict were guilty.

With the ending of the emergency on August 31 (though the ANC was still outlawed) and the release of the accused from jail on that day, the proceedings were almost back to normal. The Defense closed its case on October 7.

Phase VII. Closing Arguments and Judgment.
November 1960 - March 1961.

The Prosecution's closing argument, interrupted by several adjournments, extended to March 6. While the Defense was in the fourth week of its final argument, the Court interrupted to announce a unanimous verdict of not guilty. At this stage, the Defense had completed its legal submissions but had only just commenced its argument on the evidence. The remainder of this argument would have taken many weeks.

The Court had found it impossible, said Mr. Justice Rumpff, to conclude "that the African National Congress had acquired or adopted a policy to overthrow the State by violence, i.e. in the sense that the masses had to be prepared or conditioned to commit direct acts of violence against the State." Since the verdict was on a question of fact and not on law, the Prosecution could not appeal.

The Prosecution

The Prosecution's argument had a simplicity so grand that one can understand the exasperation with the Defense occasionally shown by Oswald Pirow, Q.C., the chief prosecutor.[6] "The essence of the crime" of high treason, said Pirow, was "hostile intent." Such intent was evident in the demands of the accused for full equality. They knew, the second indictment alleged, that to achieve the demands of the Freedom Charter "in their lifetime" would "necessarily involve the overthrow of the State by violence." Or, "in any case the accused must have known," said Pirow, "that the course of action pursued by them would inevitably result in a violent collision with the State resulting in its subversion."

The Prosecution found the hostile intent of each of the accused in his adherence to a conspiracy. The accused believed, said Pirow, that the Congress movement was "the vanguard" of the so-called National Liberatory Movement in South Africa. "The essence of the case" was the fact that the Liberatory Movement was part of an international Communist-inspired movement "pledged to overthrow by violence all Governments in non-communist countries where sections of the population did not have equal political and economic rights." The importance of communism in the trial, said Pirow, was that it illuminated the nature of the conspiracy and the conspirators' intent.

How did the Prosecution seek to prove the existence of a treasonable conspiracy? By "an irresistible inference," said Pirow, from the history of the worldwide Communist movement and the history of the extraparliamentary opposition in South Africa. Pirow admitted that the Prosecution's case was "intricate" and included "voluminous particulars"--all kinds of evidence of spoken and written words, attendance at meetings, possession of documents, and so on--many of which appeared innocent. Although the Prosecution based its case on one overt act of conspiracy, these particulars also were overt acts, done "in pursuance and furtherance" of the conspiracy, said the indictment, and necessary as proof of individual adherence to it. The "unifying element" was the Liberatory Movement. No facet of the case could be isolated from this movement, and all the activities of the accused were referable to it. In short, Pirow argued, there was no doubt about the existence

---

[6] Pirow, one of the ablest men in South African public life, had been recalled from semiretirement to lead the Prosecution. As Minister of Justice in 1929 and the early 1930's, he had been a severe opponent of left-wing activity. During World War II, which he opposed entering, he founded the New Order, an authoritarian group opposed to parliamentary democracy. He died in October 1959.

of a treasonable conspiracy if one looked at each fact in the light of all the facts.

The context in which each fact should be seen was given a comprehensive statement by Pirow in his opening address on August 10, 1959, from which the quotations above are taken. The address was, in part, an analysis of a document called the "Summary of Facts" that served explicitly as a key to the documentary evidence. By 1959 the documents had been reduced from nearly 10,000 to about 5,000, and the number of accused was down to thirty. Yet Pirow's argument and the "Summary" taken together encompassed world communism at least since 1949, the extraparliamentary movement in South Africa since 1952, other events occurring "many years" prior to the period covered by the indictment, and the activities of persons not listed even among the many alleged co-conspirators. Thus, the Prosecution linked the African National Congress, the World Peace Council, and opposition to the foreign policies of Western European countries and the United States. Also said to be Communist-inspired was the entire range of the tactics of protest, including agitation over minor grievances. All these techniques, said Pirow, were regarded by the accused as a "prelude to the ultimate revolutionary offensive."

By looking at all the facts, he declared, one also found the essential element of hostility. "Insistence upon violence," said Pirow, "runs through the case in an unbroken thread." Especially in the early stages, the Prosecution suggested that advocacy of bloody violence was not necessary in establishing hostile intent. But the Prosecution based its second indictment on such advocacy and selected thirty accused whose speeches, said Pirow, "bristle with references to the spilling of blood."

The key document was the Freedom Charter, the basic Congress manifesto. In the Prosecution's argument, however, the accused's intent illuminated the Charter more than the Charter illuminated their intent.[7] The Prosecution also relied upon

---

[7] At the close of the preparatory inquiry in January 1958, Pirow had described the Charter as Communist on its face and had treated it as the cornerstone of the Prosecution's case. The full text was printed in the first indictment. In later stages, however, the Charter was given less emphasis. During 1958, a statement of testimony to be given by a foreign expert on communism said about the Charter only that "it is most probably Communist in origin." The second indictment specified five Charter demands that were concerned mainly with public ownership and redivision of the land. Pirow's opening address in August 1959 stressed that the accused understood the Charter as "a revolutionary document," embodying aims to be achieved "in their lifetime" and therefore involving "the complete smashing of the entire State apparatus in its present form." In answering a request for particulars, the Prosecution had alleged earlier that "in their lifetime" meant five years from June 1955, the date of adoption of the Freedom Charter. The allegation was withdrawn later.

THE TRIAL AND ITS POLITICAL MEANING 19

quotations from speeches and publications that leave nothing to the imagination. In referring to motivations, that have deeper and wider roots than ideological communism, Pirow said that the accused were "inspired by communist fanaticism, Bantu nationalism and racial hatred in various degrees."

The observer of the trial faces no problem in selecting a lurid example of advocacy, whatever may be its inspiration, because one quotation stands unchallenged as the prime exhibit. This quotation is from a speech made by Robert Resha, chief of the ANC's so-called Freedom Volunteers in the Transvaal. Resha's speech can virtually be duplicated by many public speeches, but it has a sensational quality because it was made thirteen days before the arrests at a secret meeting recorded by a hidden microphone. "When you are disciplined and you are told by the organisation not to be violent, you must not be violent," Resha said, but "if you are a true volunteer and you are called upon to be violent, you must be absolutely violent, you must murder! Murder! That is all."

For illumination of intent, the Prosecution looked also at the circumstances in which words were uttered. Intent "or what could reasonably have been intended," said Pirow, could partly be determined by "gauging the probable reaction of the people who formed, for example, the bulk of the audience at meetings of the ANC." The Prosecution declared it had evidence to demonstrate that "the bulk of the country's non-European population is likely to respond more quickly, more irresponsibly, and more violently to illegal agitation than would be the case with a group whose general standard of civilization is higher" but did not introduce such evidence.

The Prosecution also looked at intent in the penumbra of circumstances of clear and present danger. Adducing such circumstances was not necessary to the legal argument, but the gravity of the charge appears to have required the justification of imminent revolt. Thus, Pirow argued that the situation at the time of the arrests was "explosive."[8] Nevertheless, intent remained of the essence. The second indictment stressed incitement and preparation for violence but did not allege that any consequences resulted that constituted an attempt to overthrow the State. Only in passing did Pirow argue in his opening address that the accused sought to exploit

---

[8] An allegation in the first indictment that the words of the accused "did in fact" promote discontent and hostility was dropped, following a request by the Defense for particulars. No evidence of violent actions that had been described in detail during the preparatory inquiry (burning of schoolhouses, wrecking of buses, and so on) was introduced during the trial. The "hostile and overt acts" alleged in the indictment constituted, as noted above, the entire range of extraparliamentary agitation and tactics.

"susceptibilities" and "passions" and "succeeded in so doing."

The Defense

The Defense confronted the Prosecution's most sensational exhibit when the secret recording of the "murder! murder!" speech was played in the courtroom on May 18, 1960, in the presence of Luthuli. Luthuli, a man of imposing dignity, denied that the speech expressed ANC policy. Earlier he had testified that since the ANC was an "omnibus" organization, whose members ranged in opinion from conservative to Communist, he was not surprised that deviationist speeches were made. But nonviolence was basic to the ANC's policy, and the ANC in practice was a restraining influence. The "militancy" of the 1949 "Programme of Action" meant work stoppages, nonviolent defiance of unjust laws, and other demonstrations intended to draw attention to African suffering. No one at the branch or national level had suggested adoption of a policy of violence. If someone had, said Luthuli, he would have opposed it on personal and practical grounds: his Christian belief and his belief that violence would be suicidal. Furthermore, the examples of India, Ghana, and Nigeria had shown him the efficacy of nonviolence.

Resha himself admitted later that he had made the speech but insisted that it was clearly outside ANC policy. When questioned by a senior member of the ANC, he had explained that he was merely trying to give an example of extreme discipline. He had sometimes expressed doubts about the ANC's policy of nonviolence, he said, but agreed with it in his calmer moments.

Luthuli's testimony supported the conception of the ANC held by the Defense: the ANC was a loosely organized movement encompassing many points of view but held together by common grievances and aspirations and officially committed to nonviolence. Subtle but sharp differences from the approach of the Prosecution distinguished the approach of the Defense to the facts in the case. For the Prosecution, African grievances had been exploited by agitators. If one was realistic, according to the Prosecution, the primary significance of African aspirations lay in the means which they implied in the circumstances of South Africa. For the Defense, African grievances were to be expected in the circumstances of South Africa, and it was realistic to accept the fact that moderate and responsible African leaders saw in the Freedom Charter, as in the Universal Declaration of Human Rights, a vision of the future. Where the Prosecution stressed the power of the accused to start a conflagration, the Defense stressed the belief of the accused in the possibility of peaceful change in response to nonviolent pressure. For the Prosecutor, the "murder! murder!" speech was a revelation of intent made by a leader in circumstances in which the usual camouflage of nonviolent affirmation was unnecessary. For the Defense, the speech was an example of irresponsible and rather incoherent demagoguery by a flamboyant individual, for whose words no accused could be held responsible in the absence of convincing evidence of endorsement. For the Prosecution, sophistication about Communist-inspired conspiracy required one to judge the complicity of an individual by relating his activity to a complex pattern of seemingly innocent facts. For the Defense, the Prosecution's attitude from the outset had been, according to I.A. Maisels, Q.C.: "Let's throw in everything the police have been able to find and see what comes out at the end." In place of vague allegations, said Maisels, each individual among the accused was entitled to particulars that informed him precisely about the nature and extent of his adherence to the alleged conspiracy.

In short, the Defense denied that the ANC was a conspiracy motivated by hostile intent. It denied the Prosecution's contention that no middle ground existed between the ballot box and treason. The activities of the accused, it maintained, were characteristic of extraparliamentary and nonviolent movements in countries that excluded a large section of the population from the political process. Such movements tended to be amorphous and undisciplined. Their leaders, more than the leaders of Western political parties, could not be held accountable for everything said by their followers. The Prosecution had selected for its case only a tiny proportion of all the speeches made. Furthermore, the grab-bag nature of the arrests, the discharge later of major leaders, and the presence of minor personalities among the thirty accused demonstrated, the Defense suggested, that no conspiracy existed.

These interpretations of the political activity of the accused underlay the argument of the Defense, but its major effort lay in challenging the Prosecution's legal argument and the significance of the evidence. The Defense also challenged the reliability of reports of speeches. In leading an expert legal course, aided by the brilliant instructions of Michael Parkington, the sole lawyer for the Defense team of advocates, Maisels acted in contrast to the course followed during the preparatory inquiry.[9] The leader of the Defense at that time had denounced the

---

[9] Maisels, perhaps the most able advocate in South Africa, was the liberally oriented leader of a Defense team, two of whose members (A. Fischer, Q.C., and V.C. Berrange) had strong Communist sympathies, which they did not disguise. Legal fees for the Defense, set far below the normal scale, were paid by the Treason Trial Defence Fund. The Fund was controlled mainly by white liberals, churchmen, and other opponents of the government. It issued the mimeographed Treason Trial Bulletin irregularly from February 1958 onwards.

proceedings as politically motivated and demanded that the law be interpreted in the framework of "democracy" rather than "fascism." Under Maisels, major legal questions such as the following were raised. What are the essential ingredients of treason in peacetime? What is meant by the policy of an organization and what facts are relevant to establish it? Can there be constructive treason? That is, does one commit treason (as the Prosecution alleged) if one performs a nonviolent act whose probable consequence is the use of violence by the State? Can one be said under such circumstances to <u>intend</u> such violence?

The Judgment

On March 29, 1961, the three-judge special criminal court announced that there was no necessity for the Defense to continue with its argument. Both sides had already argued fully, Mr. Justice Rumpff said, about the ANC's alleged policy of incitement to violence. This was "the cornerstone of the case," and the Prosecution's failure to prove this policy "inevitably meant a collapse of the whole case."

> On all the evidence presented to this Court and on our findings of fact, it is impossible for this Court to come to the conclusion that the African National Congress had acquired or adopted a policy to overthrow the State by violence, i.e. in the sense that the masses had to be prepared or conditioned to commit direct acts of violence against the State.

Nor had the Prosecution succeeded in proving "a case of contingent retaliation," that is, "that the African National Congress had adopted a plan which revealed a general expectation of violence by the State and an intention to use the masses in retaliation."

The Court did make certain findings of fact: the ANC and its allies were working "to replace the present form of State with a radically and fundamentally different form of State"; the Programme of Action "envisaged the use of illegal means" and illegal means were used during the defiance campaign; some ANC leaders "made themselves guilty of sporadic speeches of violence which in our opinion amounted to an incitement to violence"; "a strong left-wing tendency manifested itself" in the ANC during the indictment period; and the ANC frequently revealed "anti-imperialist, anti-West and pro-Soviet" attitudes. The National Executive Committee's attitude on Russia's intervention in Hungary, for example, was "pro-Soviet," said Mr. Justice Rumpff (the Committee had said, "...we reserve final judgment"); he pointed out, however, that Luthuli had personally dissented.

Mr. Justice Rumpff also found that the Transvaal Executive of the ANC, following the adoption of the Freedom Charter, had favored the replacement of the existing government by a "people's democracy," which in Marxist-Leninist thought is "a dictatorship of the proletariat, and accordingly is a Communist State." While the verdict of the three judges was unanimous, Mr. Justice Bekker in his reasons, issued some time after Mr. Justice Rumpff had read the judgment on the day the trial ended, stated that he now disagreed on this point. The Prosecution's expert witness on communism had testified that the test of whether or not a document advocated a Communist State was the presence in it of the concept of a one-party system. But the definition of "people's democratic State" in the document on which the Court's finding was based, said Mr. Justice Bekker, did not necessarily imply that a one-party system was being advocated.

In the Court's view, communism was relevant only to the issue of violence, and all the judges agreed that the Prosecution had not proved that the ANC as a national organization was Communist or that the Freedom Charter pictured a Communist State. One indication that the ANC had not adopted communism, they pointed out, was that Nelson Mandela, for example, in 1956 "foresaw a non-European bourgeois advance under the Freedom Charter."

Nor had the Prosecution proved, said the Court, that members of the Communist Party after its banning had infiltrated the ranks of the ANC and become executive leaders. The ANC allowed both Communists and anti-Communists freely to become members if they subscribed to the ANC's policy. The evidence showed that when the Communist Party dissolved itself, "a small number of executive leaders" of the ANC were already members of the party.

The ANC's demands were "far-reaching," said Mr. Justice Bekker, and could not be reconciled with "a 'mild' form of socialism." But the Court was "not convinced," said Mr. Justice Rumpff in his reasons for judgment, "that the African National Congress had acquired a policy which caused it to cross the dividing line between non-communism and communism in the spectrum of socialist belief."

Finally, with regard to the Freedom Volunteers, to whom Robert Resha had made his much-quoted "murder! murder!" speech, the Prosecution had proved the existence of such an organization, said Mr. Justice Rumpff, but it had not proved that the ANC's policy was to use the Freedom Volunteers for violent action. However, he issued a gentle reminder to the ANC on the last page of his opinion: "Of course, a political organization with members who are supposed to wear a type of uniform and who are liable to strict discipline and to the carrying out of orders without question, and who intend to bring the Government to its knees and to establish a new form of state through mass action, must not be surprised if it is regarded with suspicion by the State." Such action was not treason. Whether or not the State should allow extraparliamentary speech and pressures to continue, the Court did not say.

Results and Reactions

Without imputing motives to the government, one can appreciate the logic of the trial. By it, the accused were restricted in their movements; those who might be similarly accused were intimidated; the nature and the breadth of the extraparliamentary opposition were demonstrated at home and to the world; and the demonstration was performed in accordance with the forms prescribed by a highly respected judicial system. The government would be vindicated if it won. If it lost, it could blame defeat on the law's inadequacy and extol the meticulous standards of the judiciary. On the final decision it could base either further prosecutions or the need for new legislation.

Nevertheless, the trial was of little value to the government in its appeal to the white electorate, of doubtful value in dealing with the nonwhite opposition, and an embarrassment abroad. The Prosecution's failure to make dramatic disclosures at an early stage; the facelessness, for most whites, of the body of the accused; the tedious, complex, and protracted nature of the proceedings; and the setbacks to the Prosecution--all these made it difficult to exploit the trial politically. Whites generally found the affair a murky business, characterized either by Defense technicalities or by governmental fumbling yet probably directed at fire under the smoke. Partly because of South Africa's strict sub judice rules, the press did little to clarify the trial's issues for the public.

The trial immobilized or preoccupied many leaders of the African National Congress and diverted them from large-scale campaigns of protest and from activity against African nationalist rivals. It probably boosted the prestige of the ANC's leaders, strengthened solidarity with multiracial allies, and blurred the distinction between long-standing aspirations and Communist aims. It may have hastened the emergence of younger leaders. But by partly isolating some of the leading proponents of multiracialism and gradualism, the trial also weakened resistance to rising pressures for greater militancy.

The trial also was a drain on the energies of white liberals, who accepted the burden of obligation to provide for the defense and care of the accused. Moreover, while members of the Liberal Party sought African acceptance, whites and Indians to their left sat day after day in the unsegregated dock of the segregated courtroom. For these accused, the trial itself was a means of closer identification with the African opposition.

Despite the Prosecution's effort to stress Communist influence, hardly any foreign observers or editorial commentators accepted the trial as a justifiably anti-Communist proceeding. It failed to promote acceptance abroad of the claim of Prime Minister Hendrik Verwoerd that South Africa was the West's "best friend and most faithful ally on the African continent." Comment mainly impugned the government's motives and sympathized with the tribulations of the accused. In a judgment that was widespread, the Manchester Guardian said on November 15, 1958, that the trial was "a political trial, pursued with pitiless pertinacity."

Foreign criticism was directed at the following: the injustice of prolonged delay and uncertainty and the possibility that the trial (and successive trials) could be virtually interminable; the near-impossibility of dealing fairly with individuals in a mass trial in which no single act of conspiracy or any act of violence was alleged; the vagueness and openness to abuse of the definition of treason; the carelessness in preparing evidence and apparent arbitrariness in selecting the accused and co-conspirators; the absence of any revelations about conspiracy or any convincing evidence of attempts to overthrow the government; and the severity of personal and family hardship as a result of delay and uncertainty and inadequate provision for the accused or compensation for the dismissed. No one, to the writer's knowledge, made the charge that the trial was staged or rigged. The regularity of the trial's procedure was highly praised but sometimes was regarded as meaning little to the individual accused.

Dean Erwin Griswold of the Harvard Law School, writing in The Times of London (September 25, 1958) following his presence at the trial, summarized the difficulties of doing justice in a mass trial and passed a favorable judgment on the fairness of the proceedings. Supporters of the government occasionally cited his judgment, overlooking his description of "the underlying legal situation" as "deeply unsound."

The trial posed two far-reaching questions at the time, or, alternatively, one question seen from two vantage points. For unenfranchised and dissatisfied nonwhites, the question was: did the breadth of the Prosecution's argument leave open any extraparliamentary outlets for free speech or agitation? For whites seeking contact with these nonwhites, the question was: did the involvement in the trial of men like Luthuli and Professor Matthews mean that contact was possible only with Africans who were acceptable to the government?

Regarding the first question, the Prosecution might reply that, by requiring the existence of hostile or violent intention, it left unimpaired free speech for all, regardless of color. Although quoting the dictum of the highly respected Mr. Justice O.D. Schreiner, that "there is no intermediate course between constitutional action through the ballot box and treasonable action through illegal use of force," the Prosecution affirmed that changes "however radical and far-reaching" might be sought by "legitimate and constitutional means." Presumably such means included speech that was intended to influence those who did have the vote. For critics of the government, however, the area between ballot box and treason was a risky one to enter. Its limits could be easily constricted under the historic "intent and tendency" test, which the Prosecution followed although it talked also of circumstances of clear and present danger. Leading Africans were committed, however, to engage in what the Prosecution described as "a long and flexible process involving boycotts, strikes, civil disobedience and stoppage of work." Such pressures went beyond speech and, for the Prosecution, constituted advocacy of "revolution," which was defined as "the consummation of" the process described above.

Regarding contact with nonwhites, it appeared during the trial that all outlets and contacts not approved by the government were subject to being closed. In showing with clarity the government's attitude toward leaders like Luthuli and Matthews, the trial cast a cloud on white efforts to promote consultation with such men.

The trial, in short, epitomized the alienation of the whites in political power from Africans who demanded a share and eventually majority control of that power. The realist or defeatist saw the trial as symptomatic, epitomizing the conflict of Afrikaner nationalism and African nationalism--or, more ominous, white racialism and black racialism--as forces that cannot be separated or reconciled. The Afrikaner Nationalist, on the other hand, saw the trial as necessary, stigmatizing subversive forces that were undermining racially separate devolopment, the only policy that could prevent the submergence of whites by blacks. For the liberal or multiracialist, however, the trial was tragic. It excommunicated moderate figures with whom it was necessary for whites to consult if they were to bring about the conciliation and eventually the consent that was the only hope for multiracial peace.

Meanwhile, during the emergency of 1960, the meaning of treason in progovernment rhetoric tended to become looser. Proposals to consult with leaders of the banned ANC and PAC were characterized as traitorous. Advocacy of "intervention" by the United Nations, said a leading Nationalist newspaper, was "equal to high treason." Increasingly, the charge of treason pervaded politics, especially as foreign pressures deepened white anxiety about white supremacy and lent aid and comfort to nonwhites. But rational and uninhibited political debate was hardly to be expected in circumstances in which the stakes were believed to be life or death. A few days after Sharpeville, the Minister of Justice quoted a speaker for the ANC Youth League as having said, "De Wet Nel [Minister of Bantu Administration] must bear in mind that the day we achieve our freedom we shall charge him with high treason."

The Trial's Aftermath

Oswald Pirow said during the treason trial that the racial situation at the time of the arrests in December 1956 was "explosive." The situation continues to be chronically unstable, but control has been increasingly tightened since the end of the treason trial and the surface appears calm. The few opportunities for political expression that remained open to the extraparliamentary opposition when the Republic came into existence two months after the trial ended have not been looked upon by the government as safety valves in an explosive situation but as dangerous loopholes that needed to be closed. Long-standing and far-reaching powers for dealing with troublemakers were extended and penalties were increased by the so-called Sabotage Act of 1962. Persons banned from attending gatherings can no longer be quoted. Traditional places for outdoor public meetings have been closed. New Age and other left-wing periodicals were banned and their successors effectively stifled.

In 1963 legislation providing for repeated periods of ninety-day detention abrogated habeas corpus for political suspects or those believed to have information useful to the security police. Since then, there has been sufficient testimony in court and in sworn affidavits collected privately to indicate that in the interrogation of some African and Indian detainees ordinary police brutality has been succeeded by systematic torture, including electric shock. Some white detainees have been kept in solitary confinement in darkened cells and subjected to threatening forms of interrogation. Finally, the improved professional skill and experience of the Republic's security forces were brilliantly demonstrated on July 11, 1963. On that day, the security police provided a major setback to the underground opposition when they raided one of its main centers in a luxurious and isolated farmhouse near Rivonia, outside Johannesburg.

During the third anniversary of the treason trial's end, in March 1964, another historic trial was under way in South Africa. This was the so-called Rivonia sabotage trial in which Nelson Mandela, former president of the ANC in the Transvaal, Walter Sisulu, former secretary-general of the ANC, Ahmed Kathrada, a leader of the South African Indian Congress--all three of them among the thirty accused in the final stage of the treason trial--and seven others were on trial as leaders of the underground. They and alleged co-conspirators who had been among either the accused or co-conspirators in the treason trial--including Oliver Tambo, Robert Resha, Moses Kotane, and Duma Nokwe, all of whom are out of the country-- were accused of committing sabotage and planning violent revolution.

The time when the ANC "decided to embark upon a policy of violence and destruction" was, according to the Prosecution's opening address, "the latter half of 1961." It had formed the Umkonto We Sizwe (the Spear of the Nation), directed by the so-called National High Command, of which seven of the accused were members, and under the "political guidance" of the National Liberation Committee. In this Committee, said the Prosecution, the ANC was "completely dominated" by the Communist Party. Umkonto had recruited and trained persons in the use of explosives and in guerrilla warfare, committed acts of sabotage, received money from supporters in Africa and elsewhere and promises of all assistance from Moscow, and planned "the operation of thousands of trained guerilla warfare units," to be followed by an armed invasion by foreign powers.

Crowds like those which had attended the treason trial and the informality and mingling with the public that had marked the teatime and luncheon breaks were no longer to be seen. The accused and the courtroom were under heavy security guard, and the police reacted with suspicion to the slightest sign of communication between observers and the accused. Increasingly the police questioned nonwhites who attended the trial, and their number dwindled to only a few.

A major contrast with the treason trial period, when the State sought in one prosecution to establish the hostile intent of large numbers of accused, has been the proliferation of sabotage trials against small numbers of accused in nearly all the major centers of the Republic. According to the London Observer of June 14, 1964, in the preceding eighteen months 269 members of the ANC or of Umkonto were convicted of sabotage, and 1,162 members of the terrorist and pro-PAC Poqo were convicted. Furthermore, during the same period, 78 Africans were found guilty of political murder, and 44 were sentenced to death. In the Rivonia trial, as in many of the others, much of the evidence went unchallenged, and a major aim of the Defense was to save the accused from hanging. Their execution would have been the first for sabotage not involving loss of life.

The argument for the Defense began with a statement by Mandela similar to that which he had made in October 1962 before being sentenced to five years for having incited certain classes of workers to stay away from work and for having left the country without a permit.[10] The court in the treason trial, he said, had recognized that the ANC's policy was one of nonviolence. But at the beginning of June 1961, he and others had concluded that "all channels of peaceful protest had been barred to us" and that violence was inevitable. The ANC continued to be "a mass political organization with a political function to fulfill" and with members who had joined "on the express policy of non-violence." But it departed "from its fifty-year-old policy of non-violence to this extent that it would no longer disapprove of properly controlled violence." Umkonto was formed in November 1961, subject to the ANC's political guidance but separate from the ANC and open to persons of all races. Mandela admitted that Umkonto had planned and committed violence to property and "symbols of apartheid" and had made preparations for the eventuality of guerrilla warfare. But it had rejected terrorism, instructing saboteurs to avoid injuring or killing any person, and had not decided that guerrilla warfare was necessary.

The allegation regarding communism, said Mandela, was "an old allegation which was disproved at the treason trial." "For many decades Communists were the only political group in South Africa who were prepared to treat Africans as human beings and their equals; who were prepared to eat with us, talk with us, live with us and work with us." Cooperation between the ANC and the Communist Party had "often been close," and there was close cooperation in the case of Umkonto. The "short-term objects of Communism" corresponded with "the long-term objects of freedom movements." Therefore, he welcomed Communist assistance. But he was not a Communist--he admired the Western parliamentary system--nor had there been any change in the ANC's "ideological creed" of African nationalism, whose aims were set forth in the Freedom Charter.

---

[10] "Text of Statement by Mr. Nelson Mandela at His Trial in Pretoria on 20 April 1964," enclosure to letter from Mary Benson to the Special Committee on the Policies of Apartheid of the Government of the Republic of South Africa, United Nations General Assembly, A/AC.115/L.67, 6 May 1964.

As the time of judgment approached, the trial attracted more intense interest throughout the world than had the treason trial. Much attention centered on Mandela, who had become an almost charismatic personality. His execution, many observers feared, would mark a point of no return in the drift of Africans toward vengeance and racial hatred. On June 11, 1964, exactly eleven months after the Rivonia raid, Mandela and seven of the accused were found guilty but, on the following day, were sentenced to life imprisonment instead of death.

Their crime, said Mr. Justice Quartus de Wet, was "essentially high treason." They had committed sabotage and recruited persons for training in conventional and guerrilla warfare, but the Prosecution had not proved that Umkonto had conspired to commit guerrilla warfare. Justice de Wet accepted also the contention that saboteurs had been instructed to avoid injuring or killing any person. Regarding communism, he observed that "it does appear to me from the evidence that many, if not the majority, of the members of the African National Congress and of Umkonto also belong to the Communist Party."[11]

Branded by Dr. Verwoerd as "Communistic criminals," Mandela, Sisulu, and the other nonwhites among the accused are now on Robben Island near Cape Town. Robert Sobukwe, president of the Pan-Africanist Congress, is also on the island, in his second year of ministerially imposed detention following the completion of a three-year sentence for incitement at the time of Sharpeville. Over a thousand miles away, in a rural reserve, Albert Luthuli is adjusting to life under

---

[11] The summary of the judgment is based upon the daily edition of the Johannesburg Star, except for the quotation regarding communism, which is taken from the South African Digest, issued by the Department of Information, week ending June 19, 1964, p. 2. Neither the record nor the seventy-two-page judgment were available to the writer; therefore, the evidence for this quotation, and particularly for the generalization regarding ANC members, is not known to him.

Of the nine accused (one having been discharged at the end of the Prosecution's case), three were members of the Communist Party before it was outlawed: Raymond Mahlaba, Elias Motsoaledi, and Lionel Bernstein. (Bernstein, who had joined the party in 1939 and had been editor of Fighting Talk, was the only one of the nine to be acquitted but was immediately rearrested, to be charged later under the Suppression of Communism Act.) Govan Mbeki is a Marxist; however, in 1951, after the government had listed him as a Communist, presumably because he was on the board of directors of the left-wing Guardian, he denied that he had been a member of the party. Friends of Mbeki and of Ahmed Kathrada consider them to be Communists. Mandela and Sisulu acknowledge the influence of Marxism upon their thought and welcome Communist assistance, but they appear to be essentially African nationalists. Certainly each is too strong a personality and too independent-minded to become a Communist stooge.

a new and more restrictive five-year ban. He had known and had not disapproved of Mandela's activities, according to Justice de Wet.

Because of the virtually total alienation of independent African leadership from white authority and the spread on both sides since 1961 of a fatalistic acceptance of violence, South Africa's immediate future is unpredictable. Beneath the deceptive surface of tight control, the lines of authority are tenuous, and the situation remains inherently unstable. The decimation of African political leadership, the disorganization of mass movements, and infiltration by police informers make coordinated and disciplined resistance extraordinarily difficult. Meanwhile, according to an ANC leader outside the Republic, Rivonia spelled "the deathknell of amateurism." Well-financed and more security-conscious efforts are under way to build a cell-based underground and to recruit young Africans for political and military training. Within the Republic, police and military forces are being strengthened, while outside, foreign hostility and pressures are being mobilized. The forces of violence are moving at accelerating speeds, rapidly leaving behind all hope of racial reconciliation.

II. CHRONOLOGICAL GUIDE

Chronology

Oct. 1, 1952-Dec. 13, 1956: The period covered by the indictment.

Dec. 5, 1956:   Arrest of more than 140 persons on charges of high treason and contravening the Suppression of Communism Act. Later arrests bring the number of accused to 156 persons (and one company).

<u>Phase I. Preparatory Examination. December 19, 1956 - January 30, 1958.</u>

1956

Dec. 19-21   Beginning of preparatory examination before a magistrate in Johannesburg. Magistrate fixes bail and releases all the accused except one.

1957

Jan. 9-May 29   Preparatory examination.

June 24-Sept. 11   Preparatory examination.

Dec. 17   Withdrawal of charges against 61 persons, leaving 95.

1958

Jan. 13-30   Preparatory examination ends.

Jan. 30   All 95 are committed to stand trial on charges of high treason and contravening the Suppression of Communism Act.

Feb. 12   Withdrawal of charges against 3 persons (and one company) leaving 92 persons.

June   Indictment is issued. Lists 92 accused and 152 alleged co-conspirators (including 2 companies).

<u>Phase II. The First Indictment Argued. August 1 - October 13, 1958.</u>

Aug. 1   The trial begins before a three-judge special criminal court in Pretoria.

    One of the accused is discharged because of illness, leaving 91

    The Defense applies for the recusal of Mr. Justice Rumpff, the presiding judge, and Mr. Justice Ludorf.

CHRONOLOGICAL GUIDE 33

Aug. 4 — Mr. Justice Ludorf recuses himself. Mr. Justice Rumpff refuses to do so. Court adjourns.

Aug. 11 — Mr. Justice Bekker joins Mr. Justice Rumpff and Mr. Justice Kennedy.

Legal argument on the adequacy of the indictment begins.

Aug. 27 — The Court quashes one of the two charges under the Suppression of Communism Act and orders the Prosecution to supply additional particulars.

Sept. 15 — The Prosecution states that it will limit the indictment to the charge of high treason and the allegation of conspiracy.

Oct. 13 — The Prosecution withdraws the indictment.

Nov. 14 — The Attorney-General of the Transvaal announces that the trial will proceed against only 30 of the 91 accused and that the remaining 61 will be tried later.

Nov. 22 — New indictment is issued. Lists 30 accused and 129 alleged co-conspirators (including 2 companies).

Phase III. The Second Indictment Argued. January 19 - June 17, 1959.

1959

Jan. 19 — The trial of the 30 accused begins before the special criminal court in Pretoria.

Jan. 20 — The Court dismisses the Defense application for a change of venue to Johannesburg. Court adjourns.

Feb. 2 — Trial resumes.

March 2 — The Court rules against a Defense motion to dismiss the indictment as inadequate and refers its judgment to the Appellate Division.

April 20 — The 61 accused appear in court. They had been divided into two groups, each facing an indictment essentially the same as that faced by the 30 in January but lacking in particulars similar to those ordered by the Court since January. The Court dismisses the indictment.

June 15-17 — The Appellate Division, considering the Court's judgment of March 2, rules that it has no jurisdiction on questions of law arising from an unconcluded trial.

(Later the Prosecution furnishes the Defense with additional particulars.)

Phase IV.* The Trial Begins: Arraignment and Evidence. August 3, 1959 - March 29, 1960.

Each of the 30 accused pleads not guilty. The Prosecution presents its evidence during August 5 - November 24, 1959, and January 18 - March 10, 1960. The Defense case begins on March 14.

Phase V.* The Trial during the State of Emergency. March 30 - July 26, 1960.

Following the shooting at Sharpeville on March 21, a national emergency is declared and the African National Congress is outlawed. The accused (exept one, who has absconded) are arrested on March 30 and jailed. On April 26 the accused dismiss the Defense counsel and conduct their own defense.

Phase VI.* The Defense Back to Normal: Evidence Concluded. August 1 - October 7, 1960.

The Defense counsel return on August 1. The state of emergency ends on August 31, and the accused are released from prison. The Defense closes its case on October 7.

Phase VII. Closing Arguments and Judgment. November 7, 1960 - March 29, 1961.

1960

Nov. 7	The Prosecution begins its closing argument on the law of treason, followed by argument on the alleged conspiracy.
	Note: The trial is concluded in the case of one accused who has absconded, leaving 29.
Nov. 24 - Dec. 5	Adjournment because of Mr. Justice Kennedy's illness.
Dec. 15	Adjournment.

1961

Jan. 9	Prosecution argument resumes.
Jan. 13	Prosecution begins argument on the case against each of the accused.
Jan. 17 - Feb. 6	Adjournment because of Mr. Justice Kennedy's illness.
March 6	The Prosecution concludes its argument. The Defense begins its closing argument.
March 10	One accused dies, leaving 28.
March 29	The Court interrupts the Defense argument to announce a unanimous verdict of not guilty.

---

*The microfilm holding of the trial's record covers phases IV, V, and VI. For the detailed chronology of these phases, see Guide to the Microfilm Record, following.

Guide to the Microfilm Record

Note: The figures following the entries refer to page numbers in the microfilm of the treason trial record. See also Indexes: Numbering of Pages by Date, Volume, and Reel, below.

Phase IV. The Trial Begins: Arraignment and Evidence.

1959

Aug. 3 — The Defense makes a motion of application to quash the indictment and exception on the ground that the particular supplied by the Prosecution do not comply with the Court's order of March 2, 1959. (The Court's order had read: "The Crown is ordered to inform each accused upon which facts, speeches and documents or portions thereof as the case may be it relies in support of its inference that it was the policy or part of the policy of each of the organizations mentioned in paragraph 8 (b) and paragraphs 5 and 7 of the Summary of Facts, to use violence against the State.")

Prosecution argument. 1-19.

Defense argument (extending to the next day). 19-128.

Aug. 4 — The Court refuses to make an order on the exception or the application to quash. 128-131.

Each accused pleads not guilty. 132-136.

Statement indicating the basis of the case for the Defense. 137-139.

Aug. 5 — The Prosecution begins to submit its documentary evidence. 144.

Aug. 10 — The Prosecution's opening address. 453-521.

Aug. 11 — Admissions of fact made by the Defense. 641-644.

Aug. 20 — Additional admissions of fact made by the Defense. 1399-1401.

Oct. 11 — Mr. Oswald Pirow, Q.C., the chief prosecutor, died.

Oct. 14 — The Prosecution concludes its submission of more than 4,000 documents, testified to by more than 150 witnesses. 4614. A few documents are to be introduced later, both by the Prosecution and by the Defense.

Oct. 15 — The Prosecution begins to examine Andrew Murray, professor of philosophy at the University of Cape Town, its expert witness on communism. 4614.

Nov. 4	The Defense begins to cross-examine Murray. 5705.
Nov. 19	End of cross-examination. 6766. The Prosecution begins to re-examine Murray. 6769.
Nov. 24	End of re-examination. 6875.
	Court adjourns until January 18. 6878.
	Exhibits relating mainly to world communism, with extracts from Marx, Lenin, Stalin, Mao Tse-tung, and Khrushchev. 6879-7396.
1960	
Jan. 18	The Prosecution begins to submit evidence of meetings and speeches, announcing that it will deal first with those recorded in shorthand, then meetings recorded on tape, and finally meetings recorded in longhand. 7401. Evidence on the Congress of the People meeting of June 25-26, 1955, a separate overt act in the indictment, is to be presented at one time.
Jan. 25	The Prosecution begins its discussion of tape-recorded evidence. 7973.
Jan. 27	Playing of tape recording made secretly of meeting at which Robert Resha delivered his "murder! murder!" speech. 8141-8162 (crucial passage at 8152).
Feb. 15	The Defense argues against allowing a witness to refresh his memory by looking at a report compiled from notes. 9246-9275. The Prosecution replies. 9275-9292.
Feb. 16	Witness (S. H. White) begins to testify on Communist Party meetings that he had observed from 1929 onward. 9340. Following partial cross-examination, the Defense argues that the evidence is irrelevant and that fully testing it would require a second trial on the policy of the Communist Party of South Africa from 1929 to its dissolution in 1950. 9362.
Feb. 17	The Court rules that the witness may refresh his memory and that his evidence is admissible subject to certain qualifications. 9417-9425. The Defense requests a special entry regarding this ruling. 9430-9431.
	Witness continues to testify on Communist Party meetings. 9432-9447.
March 2	Beginning of evidence on the Congress of the People, June 25-26, 1955. 10261.
March 7	Testimony by a magistrate regarding remarks made at a criminal trial by Benson Ndimba, one of the accused, on the oath taken by Freedom Volunteers. 10467-10473. Defense later made statement that "there never was such an oath." 10674.

CHRONOLOGICAL GUIDE   37

                      Beginning of argument on the Prosecution's contention that it may lead any evidence relevant to the hostile intent of the accused, although no particulars have been given to the Defense on this matter. 10475.

March 8   The Prosecution decides not to insist on this matter. 10585-10586.

March 10   The Prosecution closes its case. 10850(c).

March 14   The Defense opens its case. 10851.

                      Beginning of testimony by <u>Dr. Wilson Z. Conco</u>, deputy president general of the African National Congress. [Underlining indicates persons who gave extended testimony in the witness stand.] 10851. Beginning of cross-examination by the Prosecution. 10897.

March 18   Beginning of re-examination by the Defense. 11306.

March 21   Beginning of testimony by <u>ex-Chief Albert J. Luthuli</u>, president general of the African National Congress. 11405.

March 28   Beginning of cross-examination by the Prosecution. 11810.

<u>Phase V. The Trial during the State of Emergency.</u>

    <u>Note</u>: Following the shooting at Sharpeville on March 21, a state of emergency was proclaimed on March 29.

March 30   Eighteen of the accused and Luthuli are arrested in the morning and are not present in court. Beginning of discussion about the status of the accused and the role of the Court. 11979.

                      Luthuli present in court. Discussion of assault upon him in prison. 11989-11994.

March 31   The Defense states that the Government, by its statements in support of the state of emergency, has made a judgment on the case. The Defense raises questions about the position of witnesses, whose testimony may lead to judicial or administrative proceedings against them, and asks about the propriety of continuing with the trial. 11996-12008.

April 1   The Prosecution opposes postponement of the trial. The Court decides to adjourn until April 19. "It is obvious to us that any witness called by the Defense may reasonably apprehend that if he is called to give evidence, his evidence may result in certain provisions of the regulations being applied to him." 12012-12045.

                      (Wilton Mkwayi, one of the accused, has disappeared.)

April 19	Discussion about official assurances to witnesses for the Defense. 12046-12083.

(The Court directs that a warrant be issued for the arrest of Mkwayi.)

Adjournment until April 26. |
| April 26 | The Defense states it is prepared to continue but describes the difficulties of conducting its case during the emergency ("knowing where persons are, whether they have been detained, whether they are out of the country or what has happened" and consulting in prison "in the presence of Special Branch men") and the belief of the accused that they cannot present their case properly. 13004-13005.

The Court decides that the difficulties are "hypothetical" and that the proceedings should continue. 13008-13011.

Duma Nokwe, on behalf of himself and the other accused, instructs the Defense counsel to withdraw from the case. Nokwe, the first African to become an advocate in the Transvaal, states that "we do not accept the bona fides of the Minister of Justice." The Defense counsel withdraw. 13011-13013.

Discussion of facilities that will enable the accused (now all in prison) to consult and prepare their defense. Accused will appear for themselves individually, but general matters will be raised by one of the accused. 13013-13021. |
April 27	Luthuli takes witness stand again and asks about his position in the light of the emergency regulations. 13025-13030. Luthuli expands on a point he made earlier. 13031-13034. (Shortly after his cross-examination began, Luthuli became ill and his testimony was limited to two hours a day.) The Prosecution resumes cross-examination of Luthuli. 13034.
May 2	(The accused raise questions about their facilities for consultation and related matters. 13111-13128.)
May 3	(The accused explain their reasons for withdrawing the Defense counsel. 13165-13170.)
May 10	(Further discussion of the conditions under which the accused are conducting their defense. 13372ff.)
May 12	(Further discussion regarding the accused. 13452-13474.)
May 17	(Discussion of the availability of Professor Z.K. Matthews as a witness. 13591-13602.)
May 18	(The Prosecution cross-examines Luthuli on Resha's "murder! murder!" speech. 13655-13663.)

| CHRONOLOGICAL GUIDE | 39 |

May 25   Cross-examination of Luthuli ends. 13818.

Additional statements by Luthuli and questions by the Court. 13819-13827.

Court adjourns until June 1.

June 1   Nokwe begins re-examination of Luthuli. 13831.

June 2   (Discussion of the conditions under which the accused are conducting their defense. 13875-13882.)

Re-examination of Luthuli ends. 13911.

Faried Adams begins examination of Mrs. Helen Joseph, national secretary of the Federation of South African Women and member of the South African Congress of Democrats and the South African Peace Council. 13911.

June 7   (Accused ask advice about the preparation of their case. 14120-14130.)

June 9   Adams ends examination of Mrs. Joseph. 14264.

A.M. Kathrada examines Mrs. Joseph. 14265-14271.

Leon Levy begins examination of Mrs. Joseph. 14271.

June 10   Levy ends examination of Mrs. Joseph. 14334.

Stanley Lollan examines Mrs. Joseph. 14334-14350.

Mrs. Lilian Ngoyi examines Mrs. Joseph. 14351-14352.

Gert Sibande examines Mrs. Joseph. 14353-14357.

S. Tyiki examines Mrs. Joseph. 14358-14364.

J. Nkampeni examines Mrs. Joseph. 14364-14366.

June 13   The accused contend that the Government's Proclamation of May 17 destroys the basis of the Court's judgment of April 26. 14367-14376.

T.E. Tshunungwa examines Mrs. Joseph. 14376-14394.

Leslie Masina examines Mrs. Joseph. 14395-14404.

Patrick Molaoa examines Mrs. Joseph. 14404-14408.

Phineas Nene examines Mrs. Joseph. 14408-14411.

Robert Resha examines Mrs. Joseph. 14411-14426.

June 13 (cont.)	The Prosecution begins cross-examination of Mrs. Joseph. 14426.
June 14	(Regarding the contention of the accused on the preceding day, the Court decides that the position has not changed. 14432-14434.)
June 21	Cross-examination of Mrs. Joseph ends. 14852.
	Faried Adams re-examines Mrs. Joseph. 14853-14871.
	The Court questions Mrs. Joseph. 14871-14888.
	A.M. Kathrada begins examination of Ismail Ahmed Cachalia, secretary of the Transvaal Indian Congress before he was banned in 1954. 14889.
June 23	Kathrada ends examination of Cachalia. 15039.
	The Prosecution begins cross-examination of Cachalia. 15040.
June 27	End of cross-examination of Cachalia. 15230.
June 28	Kathrada re-examines Cachalia. 15235-15238.
	Kathrada begins examination of Stanley Lollan, a founding member of the South African Colored People's Organization in the Transvaal. 15238.
June 29	Kathrada ends examination of Lollan. 15355.
	Adams examines Lollan. 15356-15358.
	Mrs. Joseph examines Lollan. 15358-15360.
	Levy examines Lollan. 15360-15362.
	Moola examines Lollan. 15362-15364.
	Molife examines Lollan. 15364-15367.
	The Prosecution begins cross-examination of Lollan. 15367.
June 30	(The accused say that they are recalling the Defense counsel, but since counsel will not be available until August 1, the accused ask for an adjournment until then. 15426-15430. The Court decides that it will adjourn at the end of the day until July 18. 15451-15452.)
July 18	(One of the Defense counsel is present. At his request the Chief Judge inspects the food of the accused. 15543-15546. The Court adjourns at the end of the day until July 26, instead of August 1 as requested by the Defense. 15568-15578.)

	End of cross-examination of Lollan. 15563.
	The Defense re-examines Lollan. 15563-15568.
July 26	One Defense counsel present. The Court adjourns to August 1.

Phase VI. The Defense Back to Normal: Evidence Concluded.

Note: The state of emergency did not end until August 31. The accused were released from prison on that day.

Aug. 1	Nearly all the Defense counsel are back.
	The Defense examines Simon P. Nkalipi, member of the African National Congress. 15586-15621.
	The Prosecution begins cross-examination of Nkalipi. 15622.
Aug. 3	End of cross-examination of Nkalipi. 15747.
	The Defense re-examines Nkalipi. 15747-15758.
	The Defense begins examination of Nelson Mandela, a founding member of the African National Congress Youth League. 15759.
Aug. 5	End of examination of Mandela. 15885.
	The Prosecution begins cross-examination of Mandela. 15885.
Aug. 9	Court meets and adjourns until August 15 because of illness of Mr. Justice Kennedy.
Aug. 16	End of cross-examination of Mandela. 16189.
	The Defense re-examines Mandela. 16189-16204.
	The Defense begins examination of Fred B. Ntsangani, member of the African National Congress. 16204.
Aug. 17	End of examination of Ntsangani. 16254.
	The Prosecution begins cross-examination of Ntsangani. 16254.
Aug. 18	End of cross-examination of Ntsangani. 16369.
	The Defense begins examination of Robert Resha, elected president of the African National Congress Youth League in 1953 and to the National Executive Committee of the ANC in 1955, also volunteer in chief of the Freedom Volunteers in the Transvaal. 16370.

Aug. 19   (The Defense applies for a special entry because of the "irregularity" of a series of questions asked earlier by Mr. Justice Rumpff. 16434-16435.)

Aug. 22   (The Defense explains its reasons for applying for a special entry. 16472-16524. One submission is "that the cumulative effect of the said interventions by the learned presiding Judge have created the impression that he has not approached the Defence evidence with an open mind, and has given rise to a reasonable fear in the minds of the Accused that they are not obtaining a fair trial." 16510. Mr. Justice Rumpff states that this submission constitutes grounds for recusal. 16524-16525.)

Aug. 23   (The Defense formally applies for the recusal of Mr. Justice Rumpff and begins its argument. 16591.)

Aug. 24   (The Defense concludes its argument. 16737. "...your lordship's motives and objects in questioning the witnesses are not raised in this application at all....the problem is whether the questions have created an impression that justice may not be done." 16736-16737.)

(The Prosecution comments on the Defense argument. 16737-16740. "...the applicant has indulged in a scandalous attack on the conduct of the presiding judge, in a deliberate attempt to bring him and the Court over which he presides in public contempt, to intimidate him, and to interfere with the lawful process of the Court and the due course of justice." 16738.)

Aug. 29   (Mr. Justice Rumpff refuses to recuse himself. "In my opinion the fear which the Accused say they have, that they may not get a fair trial, is an unreasonable fear and is unfounded...." 16742-16765. The Defense asks for a special entry in regard to this judgment. 16766.)

End of examination of Resha. 16801.

The Prosecution begins cross-examination of Resha. 16801.

Aug. 31   (The emergency having ended, the 29 accused--one having absconded--are released from prison and appear in court without a police escort.)

Sept. 1   (The Prosecution as a matter of urgency applies for the arrest and detention of the accused. 17077-17078.)

(The Defense objects. Discussion of the legal status of the accused during the course of the trial. 17078-17115.)

(The Court states that after the withdrawal of the first indictment, the Attorney-General allowed the conditions of bail to fall away and money was returned. When the accused appear in court on the second indictment, they were not in custody or

CHRONOLOGICAL GUIDE   43

bail and were only on summons or notice. The Court decides that it does not have authority "to order a person to be detained who in the opinion of the police, it was not necessary to arrest, or who in the opinion of the Attorney-General it was not necessary to keep in custody." Court adjourns until September 6.)

Sept. 6   End of cross-examination of Resha. 17161.

           The Defense re-examines Resha. 17161-17184.

           The Defense begins examination of Patrick Molaoa, member of the Executive Committee of the African National Congress Youth League (Transvaal). 17184.

Sept. 7   End of examination of Molaoa. 17220.

           The Prosecution begins cross-examination of Molaoa. 17220.

Sept. 8   End of cross examination of Molaoa. 17335.

           Re-examination of Molaoa. 17335-17336.

           The Defense begins examination of Gert Sibande, member of the African National Congress. 17337.

           Court adjourns until September 19 because of Mr. Justice Bekker's illness.

Sept. 19   End of examination of Sibande. 17390.

           The Prosecution begins cross-examination of Sibande. 17390.

Sept. 20   End of cross-examination of Sibande. 17463.

           The Defense begins examination of M.B. Yengwa, member of the Executive Committee of the African National Congress (Natal) before he was banned. 17464.

Sept. 21   End of examination of Yengwa. 17560.

           The Prosecution begins cross-examination of Yengwa. 17561.

Sept. 22   End of cross-examination of Yengwa. 17716.

           The Defense completes a partial cross-examination of Yengwa. 17718-17722.

           The Defense begins examination of Isaac Bhengu, first of a series of witnesses who are members of the African National Congress and are not among the accused. 17723.

Sept. 23   The Defense completes its re-examination of Yengwa. 17731-17739.

Sept. 23 (cont.)	Bhengu's testimony completed. 17745-17750.
	Testimony of David Sebolai. 17750-17759 (continued later).
	(No court on September 26.)
	Testimony of Howard Marawu. 17761-17766.
Sept. 27	Conclusion of Sebolai's testimony. 17767-17771.
	Conclusion of Marawu's testimony. 17771-17772.
	Testimony of Andries Mongwabone. 17773-17779.
	Testimony of Maxim Masheko. 17779-17783.
	Testimony of Annanias Magwaza. 17783-17790.
	Testimony of Joseph Mokamedi. 17790-17794.
	Testimony of Mrs. Jane Motshabi. 17794-17810.
	Testimony of Motsamai Ramakhula. 17811-17818.
	Testimony of Samuel Nxumalo. 17818-17822.
	(Court adjourns to October 3.)
Oct. 3	Testimony of Advocate Jack Lewsen. 17823-17861.
	Gert Sibande is recalled to testify. 17862-17864.
	The Defense begins examination of Professor Z.K. Matthews, president of the African National Congress (Cape), 1949-1955. 178
Oct. 4	(Matthews testimony is interrupted by testimony of Betty Kekana. 17931-17933.)
Oct. 5	End of examination of Matthews. 18033.
	The Prosecution begins cross-examination of Matthews. 18033.
Oct. 7	End of cross-examination of Matthews. 18243.
	The Defense re-examines Matthews. 18243-18263. (Speeches by Matthews. 18264-18307.)
	Statement by Walter Sisulu (confirming certain facts about documents). 18308-18309.
	Statement by T.E. Tshunungwa (regarding certain documents). 18309-18311.

The Defense closes its case. 18312.

The Prosecution is granted a four weeks' adjournment to prepare its argument. 18316-18322.

The Court adjourns to November 7.

III. THE ACCUSED AND ALLEGED CO-CONSPIRATORS

Chart Showing Main Changes

<u>Note</u>: This chart indicates the permutations in the lists of the accused and alleged co-conspirators at the three main stages of the trial. Regarding the designation "first string," "second string," and so on, see the note preceding the listing of names, opposite.

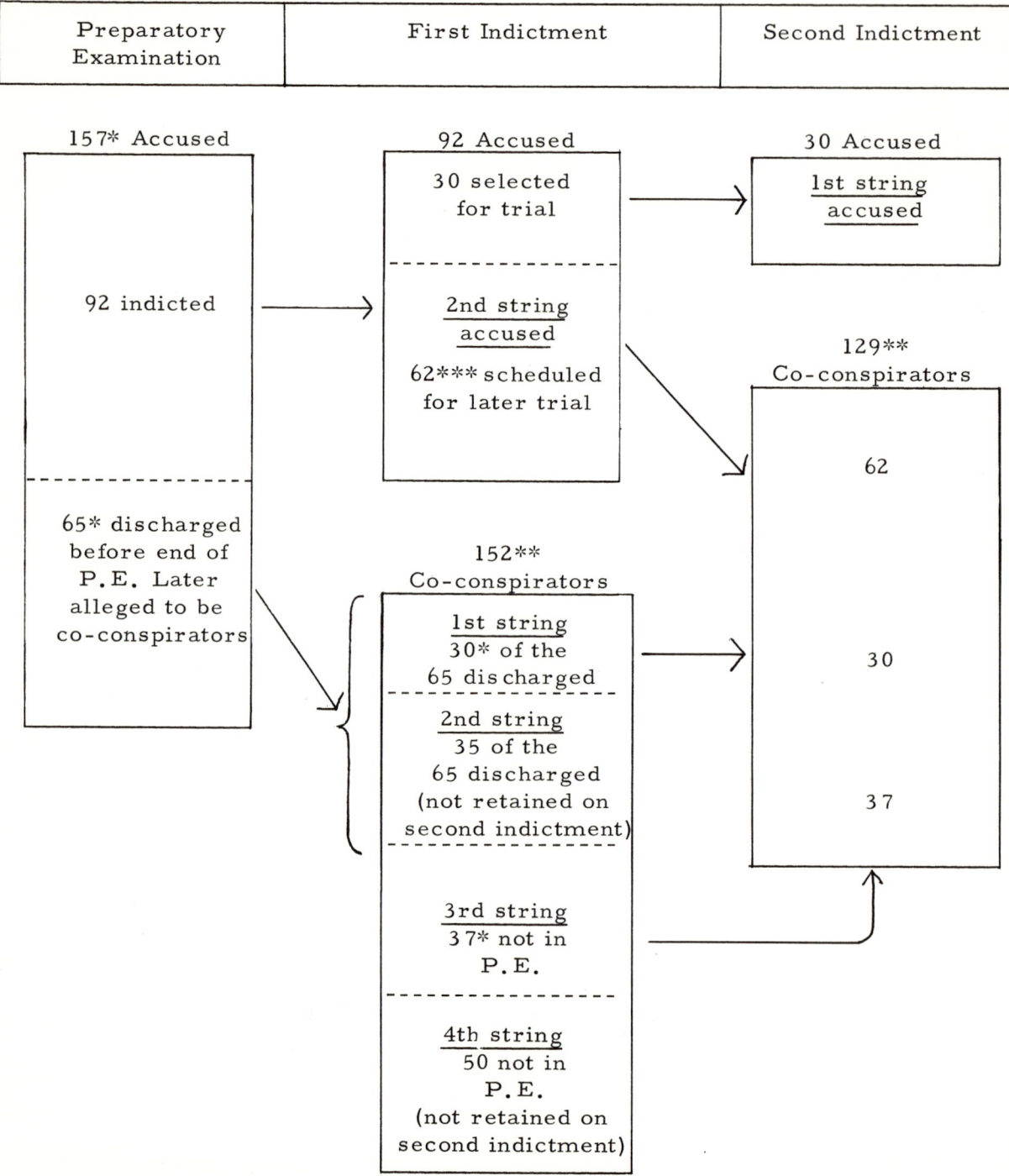

*Including one company.
**Including two companies.
***One accused was discharged because of illness. He was listed among the co-conspirators under the second indictment.

THE ACCUSED AND ALLEGED CO-CONSPIRATORS

List of Names

Note: The designations "first string," "second string," and so on are suggested solely by the positions occupied by groups of persons at various stages in the trial. See the preceding chart. The designations are not intended, it must be emphasized, to suggest the relative importance of the accused and the alleged co-conspirators in the extraparliamentary opposition. Anomalies and permutations in the lists, as noted in the essay above, can largely be explained by legal considerations of evidence and joinder and the practical difficulties of handling a large number of defendants. The Prosecution itself made clear (see its Summary of Facts, below) that some of the persons whom it considered of major influence were not among the accused or even listed among the co-conspirators.

The spelling of some names varies. The spelling used below is that which appears in the first or second indictment. This may often vary from the spelling that appears in the record. In some cases, the name has been rendered (from unofficial sources) more fully than the form in which it appears on the official list. An extraordinary feature of the listing is that a number of the alleged co-conspirators are listed by surname only.

The First-String Accused (30)

Adams, Faried
Conco, Dr. Wilson Z.
Joseph, Mrs. Helen
Kathrada, Ahmed M.
Levy, Leon
Lollan, Stanley
Mandela, Nelson R.
Masina, Leslie
Mathole, Philemon
Mayekiso, C.
*Mkwayi, Wilton
Molaoa, Patrick
Molife, Joseph
Moolla, Moosa
**Moretsele, Elias P.
Ndimba, B.
Nene, Phineas
Ngoyi, Mrs. Lillian
Nkadimeng, John N.
Nkalipi, S.
Nkampeni, J.
Nokwe, P.P. Duma
Ntsangani, F.
Resha, Robert
Selepe, Peter
Sibande, Gert
Sisulu, Walter M.U.
Tshume, Tamsanga
Tshunungwa, T.E.
Tyiki, Simon

---

*Absconded after the beginning of the state of emergency, March 29, 1960.

**Died on March 10, 1961.

The Second-String Accused (62)

Barsel, H.
Bernstein, Lionel
Beyleveld, Pieter
Bunting, Mrs. Sonia
Carneson, Fred
Chamile, Andries
Dhlamini, S.
Forman, Lionel
Hlapane, Bartholomew
Hodgson, Percy John
Horvitch, Isaac O.
Hurbans, Gopallal
Hutchinson, Alfred
Jack, Joseph
Joseph, Paul
Keitsing, "Fish"
Kepe, Lungile
Kotane, Moses
Kumalo, Jerry
La Guma, Alex
Letele, Arthur E.
Madiba, Frank
Mahlangu, Aaron
*Makgothi, Henry G.
Makiwana, Tennyson X.
Makwe, Joshua
Malupi, Sampi
Manana, P.J.S.
Mashaba, Bertha
Mati, W.
Matlou, Jonas
Matthews, Joseph G.
Matthews, Professor Z.K.
Mgugunyeka, David
Mini, V.
Mmusi, Theophilus
Modise, Johannes
Moosa, Hassen M.
Motala, Mohamed M.
Motsabi, Obed
Mquota, Temba
Naicker, Dr. G.M.
Naicker, M.P.
Naicker, Narainsamy T.
Nair, Billy
Nathie, Suliman N.
Nogaya, A.B.
Nthithe, P.P.
Patel, Ahmed E.
Peake, George
Press, Dr. Ronald E.
Seedat, Dawood A.
Seitshiro, Bennett
Sejake, Nimrod
Shall, Sydney
Simelane, Pitness H.J.
Slovo, Joseph
Slovo, Ruth (nee First)
Thompson, Reverend Douglas C.
Tshabalala, Henry
Turok, Ben
Yengwa, Massabalala B.

The First-String Co-conspirators (30)

Asmal, Mohamed
Barenblatt, Yetta
Fuyani, D.
Gumede, Archibald
Kumalo, Joseph M.
Luthuli, Albert J.
Make, V.
Malele, Elmon
Masimula, S.
Matomela, Mrs. Florence
Mavuso, John S.A.
Mfaxa, Elliot
Monanyane, Leslie
Morolong, Joseph
Mtini, John
Mtwana, Ida
Ngotyana, Greenwood
Ngwendu, William A.
Nkosi, Lawrence
Nyembe, Dorothy
Pillay, V.S.M.
Rantha, Mrs. Mary
Real Printing and Publishing Co., Pty., Ltd., represented by I.O. Horwitz
Sechoareng, Abraham
September, Reginald
Shope, Marks W.
Sibande, Cleopas
Tambo, Oliver
Tunzi, Robert
Vanga (or Banga), S.

---

*Discharged on August 1, 1958, because of illness.

THE ACCUSED AND ALLEGED CO-CONSPIRATORS

The Second-String Co-conspirators (35)

Arenstein, Mrs. Jacqueline
Baard, Mrs. Frances
Bokala, Isaac
Buza, Julius
Calata, Reverend James A.
Damons, Mrs. Stella
Dawood, Miss Assa
Dechaba, Gabriel
Esakjee, Suliman
Gawe, Reverend Walker S.
Hoogendyk, Jan
Jasson, Mrs. Christina
Lee-Warden, L.B.
Levy, Norman
Mafura, Jacob
Makgofe, Piet
Makholisa, Charles
Mashaba, July
Mashibini, Philemon
Meer, Ismail C.
Mei, Pious G.
Mkize, Mrs. Bertha
Moglakoane, Mrs. Martha
Moonsamy, Kesval
Morrison, Lionel
Mpho, Motsamai K.
Mpoza, Joseph
Ngcobo, Abednego
Poo, Jacob
Radebe, J.
Shanley, Mrs. Dorothy
Shanley, Errol
Sibeko, Archibald
Silinga, Mrs. Annie
Singh, Debi

The Third-String Co-conspirators (37)

Boikanya, P.J.
Cachalia, Y.
Competent Publishing and Printing Pty., Ltd.
Kayo, J.
Maliba, A.
Mandula, I.
Mashamaite
Matshe, R.
Mazunya
Mbeki, Govan
Mji, Dr.
Moiloa, D.
Molewa
Moola, E.
Motsabi, D.
Motsele
Mphalele, E.
Msuli
Mti, Abel
Ngqandu
Nieri, J.
Njongwe, Dr.
Padayachee, Dr.
Putini, Y.
Rampopolane
Sader
Seedat, Fatima
Sifali
Stuurman, B.
Tloome, D.
Tshuku
Tshume, B.
Tsie, Elizabeth
Vundla, P.Q.
Watson, Joyce
Watts, Hilda
Xintolo

The Fourth-String Co-conspirators (50)

Alexander, Ray
Chabanku, J.
Chele, A.
Desai
Diederich, L.
Hawthorne, Dr.
Heyman
Hlatswayo, Solomon
Joxo
Khonou, D.
Kushlik
Mahilwe
Mahlangu, J.
Mahlula
Mahope
Mamakoe
Mancaw
Mancoko
Manmokwe
Mare, J.J.
Marks
Mashaba, A.
Mathopa
Matibela, J.
Mhlaba, R.

Motsabi, J.
Motsihari
Mtuntwana
Mtwa, H.
Nazo, M.
Ngoma, V.
Ngwane
Ntshalaba
Ntstsubi
Nzo
Pello
Pendla
Petersen, A.
Routh, Guy
Sekoba
Selby, Arnold
Sililo, Dr.
Solomon, I.
Thandray
Thys
Tobias, S.
Tshabangu, Johanna
Tshume, G.X.
Weinberg, Eli
Xuma, Dr. A.B.

IV. SELECTED DOCUMENTS*

The Second Indictment

Note: The second indictment, that is, the indictment against the 30 accused whose trial began on January 19, 1959, is in reel 25 of the microfilm. It appears as Schedule No. 2, accompanying the Court's "Reasons for Judgment." The indictment is reproduced below. Three lists of names of the accused have been omitted, as noted.

Schedule A, referred to in Part B below, lists the names of 129 alleged co-conspirators. Schedule B, also mentioned in Part B, lists associations of persons or corporate bodies that are referred to in the indictment. Both schedules are reproduced in the microfilm.

Schedules C and D, referred to in Parts C and D of the indictment, respectively, and also known as the "Policy Schedule," do not accompany the "Reasons for Judgment" and are not included in the microfilm. (A copy of Schedules C and D, which consist of 85 mimeographed pages, is held by the Hoover Institution. The Hoover Institution also has a copy of Schedules C and D of the first indictment [178 and 204 printed pages, respectively] but not of the indictment itself. A copy of the first indictment is at Northwestern University.)

IN THE SUPREME COURT OF SOUTH AFRICA
(Special Criminal Court constituted in terms of
Section 112 of Act 56 of 1955, as amended.)

The Attorney-General of the Transvaal Province, who as such prosecutes for and on behalf of Her Majesty, the Queen, presents and informs the Court that: -
...[list of names of the 30 accused] hereinafter called "the accused," are guilty of the crime of

TREASON

IN THAT:

PART A.

During the period 1st October 1952 to 13th December, 1956, while owing

---

*In these extracts, the small inconsistencies that appear in the original documents have not been changed.

allegiance to Her Majesty Queen Elizabeth the Second and her Government in the Union of South Africa (hereinafter called "the State") and at or near Johannesburg, Pretoria, Bloemfontein, East London, Port Elizabeth, Durban, Cape Town, Uitenhage, Queenstown, Cradock, Kimberley, Ermelo, Evaton and other places within the Union of South Africa, the accused, acting in concert and with common purpose and in breach and violation of such allegiance, wrongfully, unlawfully and with hostile intent against the State, namely, to subvert and overthrow the State or to disturb, impair or endanger the existence, or security of the State, did

(a) disturb, impair and endanger the existence, or security of the State, or

(b) actively prepare to subvert and overthrow the State, or to disturb, impair and endanger the existence or security of the State

each accused committing certain hostile and overt acts against the State, namely the hostile and overt act laid against each of the accused in paragraph 1 of Part B of this indictment, the hostile and overt acts laid against him or her in Part C of the indictment, the hostile and overt act laid against him or her in Part D of this indictment and the hostile and overt act laid against him or her in Part E of this indictment.

PART B.

1. During the period and at the places aforesaid the accused did wrongfully, unlawfully, and with the hostile intent aforesaid conspire with each other, with the persons mentioned in Schedule A hereto, and with other persons to the prosecutor unknown, to: -

(a) subvert and overthrow the State by violence, and to substitute therefore a Communist State or some other State;

(b) make active preparation for the achievement of the objects set out in sub-paragraph (a) hereof.

2. It was part of the said conspiracy that the objects set forth in paragraph 1 of Part B above, were to be achieved by the accused in their individual capacities and/or as members, or supporters of the associations and/or corporate bodies set forth in Schedule B hereto:

3. It was further part of the said conspiracy that the objects aforesaid were also to be achieved through the instrumentality and activities of the said associations and corporate bodies.

4. (a) It was part of the said conspiracy that whilst the objects set forth in paragraph 1 hereof remained constant throughout the whole period as aforesaid, the means for achieving such objects would be determined from time to time.

(b) During the subsistence of the said conspiracy and at various times during the said period and at places to the prosecutor unknown it was agreed that the said objects should be achieved, inter alia, by the following means:

(i) sponsoring, organising, preparing for and convening a gathering of persons known as the Congress of the People for the adoption of a Freedom Charter containing, inter alia, the demands set forth in Part E hereafter, and thereafter propagating the achievement of the said demands of such Charter, adopted at Kliptown, in the district of Johannesburg, on the 25th-26th June, 1955; which said demands the accused intended to achieve by overthrowing the State by violence;

(ii) recruiting, enlisting and preparing for acts of violence, a special corps of Freedom Volunteers, being a semi-military and disciplined body whose members were obliged to take an oath or solemn pledge to carry out the instructions, legal or illegal, of the leaders of the associations of persons and/or corporate bodies set forth in Schedule B hereto; and administering the said oath or solemn pledge to Freedom Volunteers;

(iii) advocating and propagating unconstitutional and illegal action, including the use of violence as means of achieving the aforesaid objects of the conspiracy;

(iv) organizing and participating in various campaigns against existing laws and inciting to illegal and violent resistance against the administration and enforcement of such laws and more particularly -

    (a) The Native Resettlement Act, No. 19 of 1954;
    (b) The Bantu Education Act, No. 47 of 1953;
    (c) Native (Abolition of Passes and Co-ordination of Documents) Act, No. 67 of 1952;

(v) promoting feelings of discontent or unrest amongst and hatred or hostility between the various sections and races of the population of the Union of South Africa for the purpose of the ultimate violent overthrow of the State;

(vi) advocating, propagating or promoting the adoption and implementation in the Union of South Africa of the Marxist-Leninist doctrine in which doctrine there is inherent the establishing of a Communist State by violence;

(vii) preparing and conditioning the population of the Union of South Africa, and more particularly the non-European section thereof, for the overthrow of the State by violence, and inciting it to carry into effect the means hereinbefore set out.

PART C.

In pursuance and furtherance of the said conspiracy, more particularly as part of the active preparation for the violent overthrow of the State and the substitution therefore of a Communist State or some other State, the accused with the hostile intent aforesaid did during the period 1st February 1954 to 13th December 1956, being a period when all the accused were in the said conspiracy, proceed to certain meetings which were convened in pursuance of the said conspiracy and for the purposes of furthering and carrying into effect the means set out in Part B, paragraphs 4(b) (i) to (v), with the knowledge that the said meetings had been convened for the aforementioned purposes and with the intention of participating in the proceedings thereat, and did then and there attend the said meetings and make speeches for the purpose of furthering and carrying into effect the means aforesaid and/or associate themselves with such speeches, all of which appears more fully in Schedule C hereto.

PART D.

In pursuance and furtherance of the said conspiracy, more particularly as part of the active preparation for the violent overthrow of the State and the substitution therefore of a Communist State or some other State, the following accused namely: -...[list of names of 7 accused] with the hostile intent aforesaid, and in order to further and carry into effect the means set out in Part B, paragraphs 4(b)(i) to (v), did during the period 1st February, 1954 to 13th December, 1956, being a period when all the accused were in the conspiracy, write, and publish or cause to be published and/or acquire for the purpose of distribution or disseminating the contents thereof certain articles, speeches, pamphlets, or other written or printed matter as will appear more fully from Schedule D hereto.

PART E.

In pursuance and furtherance of the aforesaid conspiracy, and more particularly as part of the active preparation for the violent overthrow of the State, the following accused namely: -...[list of names of 17 accused] with the hostile intent aforesaid did attend a gathering of persons known as the Congress of the People held at Kliptown in the district of Johannesburg on the 25th and 26th June, 1955, for the adoption of a Freedom Charter, participate in the said gathering and then and there draft and adopt such Freedom Charter and pledge themselves to work together and campaign for the achievement of the demands set forth in the said Freedom Charter, which included, inter alia, the following demands:

1. Every man and woman shall have the right to vote for and to stand as a candidate for all bodies which make laws;

2. The national wealth of our country, the heritage of all South Africans, shall be restored to the people;

3. The mineral wealth beneath the soil, the Banks and monopoly industry shall be transferred to the ownership of the people as a whole;

4. Restriction of land ownership on a racial basis shall be ended, and all the land re-divided amongst those who work it, to banish famine and land hunger;

5. All shall have the right to occupy land wherever they choose, which said demands the accused intended to achieve by overthrowing the State by violence.

In the case of convictions the said Attorney-General prays for judgement against the accused according to law.

W.J. McKENZIE
ATTORNEY-GENERAL (TRANSVAAL PROVINCE)

SELECTED DOCUMENTS

The Prosecution's Opening Address

Note: This address was delivered on August 10, 1959, and appears on pages 453-521 of the microfilm record. The following extracts are from pages 453-454, 456-457, 459-462, 482, 485, and 520-521.

The case here presented by the Crown is an intricate one. The Crown will seek to bring within the scope of a single prosecution the developments of some four years or more, covering the entire country and requiring frequent reference to events in other countries; involving a score of organisations, many individuals, innumerable events, and last but not least, an excursion into the complex phenomenon known as Communism.

Before I deal with the essential facts of the case, My Lord, and the evidence to be produced by the Crown, it will be useful to refer to just a few aspects of the law of Treason applicable in the present case.

In Roman-Dutch law High Treason is committed by those who with a hostile intent disturb, impair or endanger the independence or safety of the State or attempt or actively prepare to do so. ...

In our system of law, as in the legal systems of most communities, it is not criminal to seek political reform. Constitutional changes, however radical and far-reaching, may be lawfully sought. But they must be sought by legitimate and constitutional means only. When the methods become unlawful and unconstitutional the individual using them commits High Treason. ...

The gist of the Crown's case of High Treason is that the Accused, acting in concert, and through the instrumentality of their organisations, prepared to subvert and - subvert the existing State by illegal means including the use of force and violence; and to replace the existing State with a State founded on principles differing fundamentally from those on which the present State is constituted.

My Lord, the description in terms of political science and philosophy of the precise structure and complexion of the State at which the accused aimed is not necessarily an essential element of the Crown's case. The Crown does aver, however, that such State was to be a State differing radically and fundamentally from the present State. The accused themselves described their goal to be what they called, amongst other things, "a Peoples' Democracy," a "true democracy" and so forth, and it will be the Crown's case that such a State would entail the destruction of the existing State and its machinery; its Parliament; its Judiciary; its Police Force; its Defence Force; it would involve, in a word, the smashing of the entire apparatus of State as we know it in this country today.

As to the manner and means by which the accused would achieve their aims, the Crown's case is that the accused foresaw and were bent upon no legitimate constitutional struggle for political reform, but a violent and forcible revolution or that in any case the accused must have known that the course of action pursued by them would inevitably result in a violent collision with the State resulting in its subversion. ...

The Crown alleges a conspiracy of a very wide and extensive nature. The accused and the co-conspirators have acted on a country-wide scale at different times, in different places, and by means which were not always the same. In a case of these dimensions it is obviously impossible for the Crown to demonstrate (and with respect the Crown submits that it is not necessary to demonstrate), that each conspirator participated in carrying out each detail. Nor is it necessary for the Crown to prove that each conspirator was acquainted with every other conspirator; or that each conspirator knew the exact role to be played by every other confederate. But the Crown does allege and will seek to prove that all the conspirators had in view the same criminal plan and purpose whose accomplishment was the object of all: the violent overthrow of the State, and making preparations therefor. ...

Although many of these facts, taken by themselves, may appear to be of an innocent character, the Crown will contend that if they are read together with all the other facts, it will lead to an irresistable inference that there was a conspiracy of the nature alleged by the Crown. The Crown therefore proposes to set forth the nature of the evidence which it intends to lead as proof of the facts set forth in the Summary of Facts as amplified by the further particulars. ...

The Crown relies on the fact that prior to 1952 and throughout the period of the indictment, there existed in South Africa a "National Liberatory Movement." This "National Liberatory Movement" is part of the international "Liberatory Movement" which chiefly aims at the achievement by violence in non-Communist countries of full political rights for such national groups as have not yet attained them. The Crown says that it is the duty of Communists (whose primary object is to effect a world revolution) to give active support to this movement, and that they have done so in South Africa and elsewhere, done so in countries which they regard as "colonial or "semi-colonial" countries.

In China, Korea, Vietnam, Indo-China, Kenya and Malaya the revolutionary activities of the Liberation Movement resulted in the case of each such country in actual armed conflict between the so-called "oppressed peoples" and the duly constituted authorities in such countries.

The Crown will prove that the accused, co-conspirators and the organisations mentioned in Schedule 'b' of the indictment, supported the Liberatory Movement; that they identified themselves with and expressed solidarity with the struggle of the so-called "oppressed peoples" in these countries; that they lauded the violent acts committed by the so-called "oppressed peoples" in the course of their struggle for national liberation; that they stressed that their struggle could not be isolated from the national liberation movements in the aforesaid countries, and that they advocated and encouraged the adoption of the same violent methods in the Liberatory Struggle in South Africa. The accused further considered, so the Crown will seek to prove, that the Congress Movement was the vanguard of the Liberatory Movement in this country, South Africa.

The Crown says that the essence of the case against the accused is to be found in the existence in South Africa of this so-called Liberatory Movement. This was the unifying element in the conspiracy. There is no facet in the Crown case which can be isolated from this Movement and the Crown will show that the aims and activities of the accused are always referable to this Movement. In this Movement the accused and the organisations used every grievance or local issue, even such as bus boycotts or bus fares, - issues which one would not normally associate with revolutionary activities and aims, and such issue would be made part and parcel of their struggle for so-called freedom and liberation in this country. ...

SELECTED DOCUMENTS

My Lord, the evidence will show that insistence upon violence runs through the case in an unbroken thread, and that the speeches made by the accused bristle with references to the spilling of blood. ...

In many speeches the flowing of blood is referred to in lurid terms, but the impression is sought to be created that this bloodshed would be the result of uncalled for and illegal steps even by the Police, and at the same time the speaker conveys to his audience the suggestion that the Police victims would be entitled to retaliate, thereby initiating a countrywide struggle which would result in the achievement of liberation.

The evidence will also show the Crown maintains, that the claim was made by some of the accused on various occasions, that their struggle was a "non-violent" struggle. It will be the submission of the Crown on all the evidence in the case that such non-violence slogans were used either as a camouflage, and a palpably transparent camouflage, or, perhaps more frequently than not, against such a contextual background as in fact to constitute a veiled reference or incitement to violence. ...

My Lord, then in conclusion the Court will be invited with respect, on all the evidence in the case, the Crown proposes to adduce, to arrive at the following overall picture:

1. That there existed over the period of the indictment and for some time before a countrywide conspiracy between the accused, the co-conspirators and persons to the Crown unknown to overthrow the State by violence and to substitute for it another form of State.

2. This conspiracy had its origin in the so-called Liberatory Movement, an international communist inspired and supported movement pledged to overthrow by violence all Governments in non-communist countries where sections of the population did not have equal political and economic rights.

3. The Liberatory Movement had its counterpart in South Africa where it sought to obtain its objects, inter alia, by the communist method of stirring up trouble in disputes of national and local importance. It was inspired by communist fanaticism, Bantu nationalism and racial hatred in various degrees.

4. In June, 1955, the Liberatory Movement led to the holding of the Congress of the People which formulated as a programme of action its less culpable objects.

5. All the organisations unequivocally and emphatically supported the Liberation Movement, but the most blatantly violent speeches were made by members of the African National Congress.

6. In conclusion, the accused participated fully in the activities of their respective associations and associated themselves with the attitude of the said associations in addition to committing the overt acts with which they are charged in the indictment.

The Prosecution's Summary of Facts

<u>Note</u>: This document is in reel 25 of the microfilm, where it appears as Schedule No. 3, accompanying the Court's "Reasons for Judgment." Part A, pages 1-32, sets forth the facts from which the Prosecution inferred the existence of the conspiracy set forth in Part B of the indictment. Part B, pages 32-34, sets forth the facts by which the Prosecution sought to prove the adherence of each of the accused and alleged co-conspirators to the conspiracy and their participation in it.

The extracts below are from Part A, pages 1-9, 19-22, 26-27, and 30-32.

1. (a) Before the 1st October, 1952, and during the whole period of the indictment, there existed an international movement known as the "Liberatory Movement." The said "Liberatory Movement" existed in those non-Communist countries (the so-called "colonial or semi-colonial countries") where there were nations or national groups (the so-called "oppressed peoples") which had not yet attained complete independence or the members of which had not obtained full political rights. The object of the said Liberatory Movement was the achievement of such independence for the said "oppressed peoples" and full political rights for its members, by the overthrow of the said colonial or semi-colonial states, as set forth in sub-paragraph (d) hereunder.

   (b) It was at all times and still is the duty of all Communists (whose primary object is to effect world revolution) actively to support and participate in the said "Liberatory Movement," and over the years they have in fact done so.

   (c) For many years before the 1st October, 1952, the Communist supporters of the said "Liberatory Movement," encouraged and supported the growth of "Liberatory Movements" in the said "colonial" or "semi-colonial" countries, particularly of Asia and Africa including countries such as the Union of South Africa, Kenya, China (before the establishment of the People's Republic of China), Korea, Vietnam, Malaya and Indo-China.

   (d) With the support of the aforesaid Communists "National Liberatory Movements" were formed or re-organized in the said "colonial" or "semi-colonial" countries with the object of "liberating" those countries by bringing about the violent overthrow by the "oppressed peoples" concerned of the existing regimes.

   (e) Throughout the period of the indictment such a "National Liberatory Movement" existed in the Union of South Africa, as will appear more fully hereafter.

2. (a) The establishment in Paris, in 1949, of the World Peace Council, with its executive council, the Bureau of the World Peace Movement, which controls the policy and conducts the activities of the World Peace Council under direction of the government of Soviet Russia (hereinafter referred to as the U.S.S.R.).

SELECTED DOCUMENTS   59

- (b) (i) The object of the World Peace Council has been to propagate the policies and interests of the U.S.S.R. and other Communist countries, and to defend the actions and activities of the U.S.S.R. particularly in regard to matters of international policy.
  - (ii) It was also an object of the World Peace Council to emphasize the indivisibility of the struggle for peace and the struggle for liberation and to support the said Liberatory Movement, more particularly the National Liberatory Movement in the Union of South Africa.
  .....

3. The facts set forth in the evidence of Professor Murray at the Preparatory Examination, pages 4523 to 4644, and in the statements of certain Bochenski, copies of which have been served on the accused.

4. (a) The existence in the Union of South Africa until 1950, of the South African Communist Party, which was affiliated to the Communist Party of the U.S.S.R.

   (b) The aims, purposes and objects of the South African Communist Party included the following, namely:
   - (i) The overthrow of the South African State and the establishment in its stead of a Communist State;
   - (ii) support for the aforesaid Liberatory Movement and the promotion and encouragement of a National Liberatory Movement in South Africa;
   - (iii) support of all international communist-sponsored organisations such as the World Peace Council, the World Federation of Trade Unions, the World Federation of Democratic Youth, the Women's International Democratic Federation;
   - (iv) The propagation of Communism and the undermining of the South African State to prepare for the overthrow thereof;

   (c) During 1950 the South African Communist Party was dissolved. Thereafter the associations set forth in paragraphs 5 and 7 hereof were infiltrated by members of the defunct South African Communist Party, and such persons were appointed to executive positions in the said associations.

5. The existence prior to the 1st October 1952 and during the whole period of the indictment of the following associations or corporate bodies, including all their local and provincial branches within the Union, (hereafter referred to as "organisations") namely:
   The African National Congress, with its various sections.
   The South African Indian Congress.
   The Natal Indian Congress.
   The Transvaal Indian Congress.
   The Transvaal Indian Youth Congress.
   The Natal Indian Youth Congress.
   The South African Society for Peace and Friendship with the Soviet Union (formerly known as the Friends of the Soviet Union or F.O.S.U.).
   The Transvaal Peace Council.

6. (a) The formation during or about July, 1951, by the Executive Committees of the A.N.C. and the S.A.I.C. of a Joint Planning Council to co-ordinate the efforts of the A.N.C. and the S.A.I.C. to organise support for the "National Liberatory Movement" in South Africa, by mass action.

(b) The acceptance by the A.N.C. and the S.A.I.C. of a recommendation by the said Joint Planning Council, to embark on a mass campaign for the defiance of so-called "unjust laws," namely Pass Laws, Stock Limitation Regulations, the Separate Representation of Voters' Act, the Suppression of Communism Act, and the Bantu Authorities Act.

(c) The formation during or about June 1952, by the Executive Committees of the A.N.C. and the S.A.I.C. of the National Action Committee and the National Volunteer Board, both of which consisted of representatives of the A.N.C. and the S.A.I.C., having the functions of controlling, directing, and co-ordinating the activities of the A.N.C. and the S.A.I.C. in waging a campaign of defiance of the so-called unjust laws, which was launched on the 26th of June 1952.

(d) The appointment of the following persons, namely Y.M. Dadoo, President of the S.A.I.C.; M. Kotane, Member of the National Executive of the A.N.C.; J.B. Marks, Member of the National Executive and President of the A.N.C. (Tvl) [Transvaal]; D.W. Bopape, Secretary of the A.N.C. (Tvl); and J. Ngwevela, Chairman of the Cape Regional Committee, all of whom had been members of the South African Communist Party, as the first volunteers in the said defiance campaign, and the recruitment on a large scale throughout the Union of South Africa of volunteers to defy the said laws.

(e) The waging by the A.N.C. and the S.A.I.C. during the period 26th June 1952 to January 1953, on a country-wide scale throughout the Union of South Africa of a campaign of defiance of the so-called unjust laws.

7. The formation and existence of the following associations of persons or corporate bodies, including all their local and provincial branches and organisations within the Union, (hereafter referred to as "organisations") as from the dates set opposite their respective names, namely:

The South African Peace Council - 21.8.1953.
The South African Congress of Democrats - 8.9.1953.
The South African Coloured Peoples Organisation - October 1953.
The South African Indian Youth Congress - December 1953.
The Federation of South African Women - April 1954.
The South African Congress of Trade Unions. - 6.3.1955.

8. (a) It was part of the policy of each of the organisations mentioned in paragraphs 5 and 7 above to achieve any one or more of the following objects, namely:

(i) to subvert and overthrow the State;

(ii) to make active preparation for a violent revolution against the State;

(iii) to disturb, impair or endanger the security or authority of the State;

(iv) to hinder and hamper the State in the enforcement of laws and the maintenance of peace and order;

(v) to oppose and resist the authority of the State, and in particular the power of the State to make and enforce laws.

SELECTED DOCUMENTS 61

      (vi) to support the "Liberatory Movement" (hereinbefore described) and more particularly the "National Liberatory Movement" in the Union of South Africa;

     (vii) to establish a communist state or some other state in the place of the present state;

    (viii) to form a so-called "United Front" with the other organisations for the purpose of co-ordinating the activities of the said organisations and their members, and to enlist, as far as possible, the support of any other organisations or persons, in furtherance of their policies set out herein.

. . . . .

9. Each of the aforesaid organisations sought to advance and implement its policy aforesaid:

. . . . .

  (f) through the activities of the National Action Council of the C.O.P. (hereinafter referred to as N.A.C.C.O.P.) and the National Consultative Committee (hereinafter referred to as N.C.C.) as set out in paragraphs 10 and 11 hereafter;

  (g) by organising study-classes for the purpose of indoctrinating their members with the principles of Marxism-Leninism and teaching them the necessity for revolutionary tactics in South Africa;

  (h) by exploiting the local grievances in connection with bus fares, rents, housing and the non-employment of Natives in shops serving predominantly Native localities with the object of obtaining their support for the achievement and implementation of the policies of the organisations aforesaid.

10. (a) The formation during or about March 1954 by the A.N.C., S.A.I.C., S.A.C.O.D. and S.A.C.P.O. of N.A.C.C.O.P. and the establishment of the various provincial, regional and local action councils of the C.O.P., consisting of representatives of each of the aforesaid organisations with the object of:

    (i) co-ordinating the activities of the said organisations and of their members, to provide for the common policy, strategy, tactics, and co-operation, and

    (ii) sponsoring, planning and promoting joint activity and joint campaigns by the aforesaid organisations and by their members so as to more effectively implement the aforesaid policy of said organisations.

  (b) In 1955 representatives of S.A.C.T.U. became members of N.A.C.C.-O.P. and the said action councils; in the same year representatives of the C.T.P.C. became members of the Cape Western Action Council of the C.O.P.

  (c) The said organisations through their representatives participated in the activities of N.A.C.C.O.P., and the aforesaid provincial and regional and local councils of the C.O.P., as from the date of their membership, such activities consisting <u>inter alia</u> of:

- (i) meeting together from time to time during the period March 1954 to about August 1955 at Johannesburg, Pietermaritzburg, Fraser Station, Durban, Port Elizabeth, Cape Town and other places to the prosecutor unknown with the object of promoting and co-ordinating the activities of the said constituent organisations, particularly in regard to:

    - (aa) the convening of and preparations for the Congress of the People at Kliptown, Johannesburg, on the 25th and 26th. June, 1955, for the adoption of a Freedom Charter;

    - (bb) the linking of various campaigns set afoot and organised by the said organisations such as the campaign against the Bantu Education Act, the Western Areas Removal Campaign, the Campaign against Passes, with the campaigns for the preparations for the C.O.P. and the achievement of the aims of the Freedom Charter, which included <u>inter alia</u> the demands set forth in paragraphs 1 to 5 in Part $\overline{\text{E}}$ of the Indictment.

    - (cc) the activities of the special militant corps of Freedom Volunteers.

- (ii) organising and convening public meetings throughout the Union of South Africa in support of a Congress of the People and the adoption of a Freedom Charter.

- (iii) drafting, printing or causing to be printed, publishing or causing to be published, distributing or causing to be distributed brochures, bulletins, pamphlets, circulars, such as: -

    . . . . .

- (iv) organising and conducting study classes more particularly for Freedom Volunteers, at which lectures entitled "The World we live in" "The Country we live in" and "Change is needed" were delivered.

(d) The Congress of the People held at Kliptown on the 25th to the 26th of June, 1955, and the adoption of the Freedom Charter, as alleged in Part E of the indictment.

11. (a) The formation in August 1955, by A.N.C., S.A.I.C., S.A.C.P.O., S.A.C.O.D., and S.A.C.T.U. of the National Consultative Committee and the various provincial consultative committees, consisting of representatives of A.N.C., S.A.I.C., S.A.C.P.O., S.A.C.O.D. and S.A.C.T.U. and at a later stage also representatives of F.S.A.W., with the object of:

- (i) co-ordinating the activities of the said organisations and of their members, to provide for common policy, strategy, tactics and action, and

(ii) sponsoring, planning and promoting joint activity and joint campaigns by the aforesaid organisations and by their members, so as to more effectively achieve and bring into effect the aforesaid policy of the said organisations subsequent to the adoption of the Freedom Charter at Kliptown, Johannesburg, on the 25th to 26th June, 1955.

. . . . .

12. The formation and existence as from February 1954 of the Fighting Talk Committee, being an association of persons whose members included the co-conspirators, Ruth Slovo, L. Bernstein and Yetta Barenblatt. The names of the other members of the said committee are to the Prosecutor unknown. The said committee through its members published and distributed a monthly bulletin called "Fighting Talk" as from March, 1954, and in the said bulletins the policies and activities of the aforesaid organisations and their members were advocated, propagated, supported and defended.

13. The formation and existence as from June 1953 of the Liberation Committee, being an association of persons whose members included the co-conspirators, P.J. Hodgson, S. Bunting and D. Tloome. The names of the other members of the said committee are to the Prosecutor unknown. The said committee through its members published and distributed a monthly bulletin called "Liberation" as from June 1953, and in the said bulletin the policies and activities of the aforesaid organisations and their members were advocated, propagated, supported and defended.

14. The formation and existence as from February 1955, of the Call Committee, being an association of persons, whose members included the co-conspirators, S. Dhlamini and N.T. Naicker. The names of the other members of the said committee are to the Prosecutor unknown. The said committee through its members and through the N.I.C. published and distributed a monthly bulletin called "The Call" as from February 1955, and in the said bulletins the policies and activities of the aforesaid organisations and their members are advocated, propagated, supported and defended.

. . . . .

16. (a) The formation and existence as from 26.10.1952 of a private company namely "Competent Publishing and Printing (Pty). Ltd." whose directors and/or servants included the co-conspirators Fred Carneson, a director, and Lionel Forman, a servant, as editor. The said company published and distributed a weekly news-paper called "Advance" as from 26.10.1952 to 21.10.1954, in which the policies and activities of the aforesaid organisations and their members were advocated, propagated, supported, and defended.

(b) The formation and existence as from March 1953 of a private company namely "Real Printing and Publishing Company (Pty.) Ltd.," whose directors and/or servants included the co-conspirators Fred Carneson, director and/or servant as manager, I.O. Horvitch, director and/or servant, Lionel Forman, servant, as editor, and R. Slovo, servant. The said company published and distributed the weekly newspaper called "New Age" as from 28.10.1954 to 13.12.1956, in which the policies and activities of the aforesaid organisations and their members were advocated, propagated, supported and defended.

. . . . .

Preliminary Statement by the Defense

"It has already become apparent during the preliminary stages of this case that the central issue is the issue of violence. While no admissions are made in regard to any of the Crown's allegations, the Defence case will be that it was not the policy of the African National Congress or any of the other organisations mentioned in the indictment to use violence against the State. On the contrary, the Defence will show that all these organisations had deliberately decided to avoid every form of violence, and to pursue their ends by peaceful means only. The Defence will rely for its contentions as to the policies of these organisations upon their constitutions, the resolutions taken by them at their conferences and the pronouncements of their responsible national leaders. If necessary these leaders will be called as witnesses for the Defence. The Defence will place before this Court the material relating to these organisations from which their policies might normally be expected to be deduced. In its indictment the Crown has relied upon certain speeches. Most of them by persons of minor importance, which may seem to suggest the existence of a policy of violence. [sic] Insofar as such speeches were in fact made in the terms alleged, the Defence will say that they may have represented the notions of individuals and not the policy of the organisations."

Admissions Made by the Defense

The defence admits:

1. That during 1952 the A.N.C. and S.A.I.C. decided to conduct a campaign for the Defiance of Unjust Laws, and did conduct a campaign, involving the deliberate contravention of certain laws by the way of protest and in order to bring about political and social changes in South Africa.

2. That between March 1954 and July 1955, the A.N.C., S.A.I.C., S.A.C.O.D. and S.A.C.P.O. were represented upon the National Action Council for the C.O.P. and supported the organisation of this C.O.P.

3. That the campaign for the C.O.P. supported by the above-mentioned organisations, involved the collection of demands for inclusion in the Freedom Charter, and culminated on 26th June 1955, in the adoption of the Freedom Charter at the C.O.P. in Kliptown.

4. That after July 1955, the A.N.C., S.A.I.C., S.A.C.O.D., S.A.C.P.O. and S.A.C.T.U. were represented upon the National Consultative Committee and supported the publication and popularisation of the Freedom Charter.

5. That the A.N.C., S.A.I.C., S.A.C.O.D., S.A.C.P.O., S.A.C.T.U. and F.S.A.W. were opposed to the enactment and/or provisions of the Group Areas Act, the Bantu Education Act and Natives Resettlement Act and the laws relating to the carrying of passes by Africans.

6. That during the years 1954, 1955 and 1956, the A.N.C. conducted campaigns against the Bantu Education Act, the Natives Resettlement Act and the laws relating to the carrying of passes by Africans, in the course of which it advocated

(a)   the boycott of Bantu schools by the pupils thereof,

(b)   that the inhabitants of the so-called Western Areas of Johannesburg should not voluntarily leave their homes,

(c)   that African women should not voluntarily apply for reference books.

7. That the A.N.C., S.A.I.C., S.A.C.O.D., S.A.C.P.O., S.A.C.T.U. and F.S.A.W. were strongly opposed to the apartheid policy and legislation of the government of the Union of South Africa and denounced the government in vigorous terms.

8. That the A.N.C., S.A.I.C., S.A.C.O.D., S.A.C.P.O., S.A.C.T.U. and F.S.A.W. criticised the present constitution of the Union of South Africa.

9. That the A.N.C., S.A.I.C., S.A.C.O.D., S.A.C.P.O., S.A.C.T.U. and F.S.A.W. demanded the substitution of a new and radically different government and in particular advocated

(a)   a system of government based on universal adult suffrage,

(b)   the abolition of all forms of racial discrimination.

10. That the A.N.C., S.A.I.C., S.A.C.O.D., S.A.C.P.O., S.A.C.T.U. and F.S.A.W. accepted the view that extra-parliamentary activity should be resorted to, and advocated and carried on extra-parliamentary, activity.

11. That during the years 1954, 1955 and 1956, the A.N.C., S.A.I.C., S.A.C.O.D., and S.A.C.P.O. recruited or supported the recruitment of a body of persons known as the Freedom Volunteers.

12. That the A.N.C., S.A.I.C., S.A.C.O.D., and S.A.C.P.O. criticised the colonial system and sympathised with the efforts of colonial countries to obtain self-government.

13. That the expressions by the A.N.C., S.A.I.C., S.A.C.O.D., S.A.C.P.O., S.A.C.T.U. and F.S.A.W. of their admitted policies were often vehement and repetitive.

14. (a) That all the above named organisations cooperated with one another generally in the policies and activities above set forth insofar as such activities took place during the period of existence of each organisation.

(b) That the A.N.C.Y.L. and A.N.C.W.L. similarly cooperated with the A.N.C.

(c) That the T.I.C. and N.I.C. were constituent parts of the S.A.I.C.

(d) That the T.I.Y.C. and N.I.Y.C. similarly cooperated with the T.I.C. and N.I.C. respectively.

Additional Admissions Made by the Defense

1. That the Defiance Campaign was directed against the following laws, namely,

    (a) Pass Laws;

    (b) Stock Limitation Regulations.

    (c) Group Areas Act.

    (d) The Separate Representation of Voters Act.

    (e) The Suppression of Communism Act.

    (f) The Bantu Authorities Act.

2. That the S.A.I.C. and A.N.C. formed a National Volunteer Board as part of their activities in the Defiance Campaign.

3. That the Defiance Campaign was carried on in several parts of South Africa from the 26th June, 1952 to December 1952.

4. That N.A.C.C.O.P. established various provincial Regional and local action councils, consisting of representatives of the constituent organisations, namely the following: ---

    (a) Natal Action Council.

    (b) Transvaal Action Council.

    (c) Johannesburg, Natal Midlands, Cape Eastern and Cape Western Regional Committees.

5. That the object of the N.A.C.C.O.P. was the co-ordination of the activities of the organisations in their sponsorship and organisation of the C.O.P.

6. That the provincial, regional or local councils of N.A.C.C.O.P. organised meetings at various places in South Africa in support of the C.O.P.

7. That the C.O.P. campaign was conducted in many parts of South Africa.

8. That various joint consultative provincial and regional committees were established by the organisations.

9. That meetings of the N.C.C. or the provincial or regional committees were held to discuss:--

(a) Publicising the Freedom Charter,

(b) Passes.

10. That the campaigns against the laws referred to in paragraph 6. of the first set of admissions, constituted part of the policy of extra-parliamentary activity.

11. That the said campaigns were conducted in many parts of South Africa.

12. That these campaigns were regarded as part of the general activity of the organisations.

13. That the organisations advocated extra-parliamentary action as a means of achieving the change of government desired by them, as set out in paragraph 9. of the first set of admissions.

14. That Chief A.J. Luthuli, on behalf of the A.N.C., called for 50,000 Freedom Volunteers and that the other organisations supported his appeal.

15. That the T.I.Y.C. and N.I.Y.C. had all the policies and participated in all the activities which have been admitted with reference to the S.A.I.C. and that the T.I.Y.C. and N.I.Y.C. co-operated with the other organisations referred to in the admissions.

Judgment of the Special Criminal Court
Regina vs. F. Adams and Others

The Court stated on that day that it would submit reasons for its decision later. These appear at the end of reel 25 of the microfilm. Mr. Justice Rumpff's opinion is 168 pages long; Mr. Justice Kennedy's, 88 pages; and Mr. Justice Bekker's, 169 pages. Mr. Justice Bekker's opinion includes a short history of the African National Congress.

The opinions are accompanied by nineteen schedules (the first part of reel 25). Schedule No. 1 is the judgment of March 29, 1961. Schedule No. 2 is the second indictment. Schedule No. 3 is the Prosecution's Summary of Facts. Schedule No. 4 is the admissions of fact made by the Defense. Schedules numbered 5, 7-9, 12-15, and 19 are documents that are included in the List of Selected Documents, below. The remaining schedules include a 36-page summary of evidence by the Prosecution's expert witness on communism (Schedule No. 6) and excerpts from Fighting Talk, Liberation, Advance, New Age, and African Lodestar.

Rumpff, J.:

We have considered the evidence put before the Court and the arguments addressed to us on behalf of the Defence.

The further arguments to be addressed to us by the Defence on the contents of a number of reported speeches and on the policy of the organisations other than the African National Congress, do not appear to us to affect materially the consideration of the question whether or not the Prosecution has discharged the onus which rests on it in connection with the policy of violence attributed to the African National Congress, and which alleged policy is the cornerstone of the case for the Prosecution. If the case fails against the African National Congress it must fail against the other organisations. The policy of the African National Congress has been argued fully by the Prosecution and by the Defence, and we do not think it necessary for the Defence further to address us.

We also wish to announce that after full consideration of the issues in this case, we have arrived at a unanimous verdict. In the normal course of events we would not have delivered our verdict without at the same time fully setting out our reasons therefor, but in view of the mass of evidence with which we have to deal the formulation of our reasons will of necessity take a considerable time. This consideration, and the fact that this case has already consumed some years of hearing, have induced us to announce our verdict together with such essential findings of fact as have been arrived at by us on the evidence in the case. Written reasons for our verdict will in due course be handed to the Registrar of this Court.

I shall now proceed to deal with our verdict, and the accused may remain seated.

The accused are charged with treason. They have pleaded not guilty.

The first overt act of treason laid against all the accused in the indictment is a conspiracy to overthrow the State by violence. Against each accused further overt acts are laid, and these acts are said to have been committed in pursuance of the conspiracy.

The case for the Prosecution is not that the accused came together and entered into a treasonable agreement. The case for the Prosecution is that during the indictment period, i.e. from the 1st October, 1952, to the 13th December, 1956, a period of about four years, a number of organisations in South Africa, including the African National Congress, the South African Indian Congress, the South African Congress of Democrats, and the South African Coloured Peoples Organisation, had a policy to overthrow the State by violence; that these organisations co-operated with each other to achieve their common object, and that for that purpose an alliance was established, which for convenience sake has been referred to as the Congress Alliance, with the African National Congress as the senior and dominant partner.

The accused are said to have conspired because they took an active and leading part in the activities of the organisations of which he or she was a member, with full knowledge of and support for the policy of such organisations.

In order to prove the existence of the treasonable conspiracy the Prosecution had to prove the violent policy of the Congress Alliance. It also had to prove the adherence of each of the accused to the conspiracy.

It is conceded by the Prosecution that if it fails to prove the treasonable conspiracy there is no case against any of the accused.

In regard to the alleged policy of violence the indictment alleges that the intention was to overthrow the State by violence, and to substitute for it a Communist State or some other State, and that the means by which the overthrow would be achieved were agreed to be the following:-

(1) The convening of a gathering of persons known as the Congress of the People, for the adoption of a Freedom Charter, containing certain demands, which demands the accused intended to achieve by overthrowing the State by violence.

(2) By recruiting and preparing for acts of violence a special Corps of Freedom Volunteers.

(3) Advocating and propagating unconstitutional and illegal action including the use of violence.

(4) Organising, and participating in, various campaigns against existing Laws, and inciting to illegal and violent resistance against the administration and enforcement of such Laws, more particularly the Native Resettlement Act, No. 19 of 1954, the Bantu Education Act, No. 47 of 1953, and the Natives' (Abolition of Passes and Co-Ordination of Documents) Act, No. 67 of 1952.

(5) Promoting feelings of discontent or unrest amongst and hatred or hostility between the various races of the Union.

(6) Propagating the adoption in the Union of the Marxist-Leninist doctrine, in which doctrine there is inherent the establishing of a Communist State by violence.

(7) Preparing and conditioning the population of the Union, more particularly the non-European section, for the overthrow of the State by violence, and inciting it to carry into effect the agreed means.

The indictment and the further particulars supplied suggest, in the main, a policy of incitement to violence during the period of the indictment.

After all the evidence had been heard, and at one stage during the argument in reply to questions put by the Court, the Prosecution specifically stated that on the evidence its case against the African National Congress was that it intended to organise the masses against the State, and that through a process of campaigns, stay-at-homes and strikes it would make its demands; that if those demands were not acceded to, and if the circumstances were favourable in the sense that the masses were sufficiently politically conscious, it would organise a nation-wide strike which would be the final clash between the people and the State; that the African National Congress expected violence from the State to suppress the attack against it, and that the African National Congress intended at that stage actively to retaliate.

The Prosecution also stated that in regard to the removal from the Western Areas its case was that the African National Congress was reckless in regard to whether violence ensued or not, and that as regards the Freedom Volunteers the case against them was not that they were expected to commit violence during the period of the indictment, but in the ultimate end when the order would be given to be violent.

It was submitted by the Defence that the case thus described was not the case set out in the indictment, that the indictment and the Further Particulars suggest a policy of direct violence, and that the case described by the Prosecution during argument was a case of contingent retaliation.

We shall return to the submissions made by the Prosecution later, but because of the view we take of all the evidence put before the Court it is not necessary to consider whether the indictment covers the case suggested by the Prosecution, nor is it necessary to deal with the arguments addressed to us by the Defence on the two witness rule, and on the legal nature of an overt act of treason.

In our opinion the evidence proves the following:-

1(a) That the African National Congress and all the other organisations mentioned in the indictment, as well as the present accused, were working together to replace the present form of State with a radically and fundamentally different form of State, based on the demands set out in the Freedom Charter which included inter alia the following:

1. "Every man and woman shall have the right to vote for and to stand as candidate for all bodies which make laws.

2. The national wealth of our country, the heritage of all South Africans, shall be restored to the people.

3. The mineral wealth beneath the soil, the banks and monopoly industry, shall be transferred to the ownership of the people as a whole.

4. Restriction of land ownership on a racial basis shall be ended, and all the land redivided amongst those who work it, to banish famine and land hunger."

1(b) That prior to the adoption of the Freedom Charter the Congress Alliance sought to obtain from its members and others "demands of the people," which were presented at the Congress of the People on the 25th and 26th of June, 1955, and which formed the basis of the Freedom Charter.

1(c) That as part of its campaign to obtain the necessary demands from the people, and also to raise the political consciousness of the people, the Congress Alliance, through its member organisations, arranged for the holding of meetings whereat various members addressed the public. It also made use of propaganda material and arranged for the distribution and use of various lectures and lecture notes. The general trend of the speeches made and of the propaganda and the lectures and lecture notes, was to condemn the system of Government in South Africa, and to extoll the virtues and advantages of a State described in varying terms as People's

Democracy or True Democracy, and to place the need for the recognition of the principle of general and unqualified franchise in the forefront. The Defence conceded in argument that some of the lectures referred to, contained traces of Communist influence.

1(d) That it has not been proved that the form of State pictured in the Freedom Charter is a Communist State.

1(e) That after the adoption of the Freedom Charter, the Transvaal Executive of the African National Congress propagated the view that "the African National Congress aimed to replace this Government of the few with a Government of people's democracy. In a people's democratic State the power of State will be exercised by the people, i.e., by the working people of all colours, together with all other democratic classes who will work for the changes set out in the Freedom Charter. This will be a Government of the people as a whole, of the present oppressed and exploited classes used to achieve their maximum well-being, and to prevent the few exploiters from regaining State power."

1(f) The contention of the Defence that the State advocated by the Transvaal Executive of the African National Congress is not a dictatorship of the proletariat is rejected, and we are of the opinion that the type of State as seen by the Transvaal Executive of the African National Congress is a dictatorship of the proletariat, and accordingly is a Communist State, known in Marxism-Leninism as a people's democracy.

1(g) That it was the policy of the African National Congress that Communists and anti-Communists could freely become members of the African National Congress, provided they subscribed to the policy of the African National Congress, and that some responsible Executive leaders of the African National Congress were members of the Communist Party before it was banned in 1950. There is no evidence to support the allegation of the Prosecution that there was infiltration by members of the former Communist Party into the ranks of the African National Congress.

1(h) That the African National Congress took up the attitude that Communists were free to spread their ideologies amongst members of the African National Congress, provided they honoured the policy of the African National Congress.

1(i) That in the indictment period a strong left-wing tendency manifested itself in the African National Congress.

1(j) That it has not been proved that the African National Congress had become a Communist organisation.

1(k) That the issue of Communism is relevant in this case to the issue of violence, and that on the evidence as a whole the Prosecution has failed to prove that the accused had personal knowledge of the Communist doctrine of violent revolution, or that the accused propagated this doctrine as such.

2. That the means to be employed for the achievement of the New State were those decided upon by the African National Congress in its duly adopted and official 1949 Programme of Action.

3. The preamble to the Programme of Action reads:

> "The fundamental principles of the Programme of Action of the African National Congress are inspired by the desire to achieve national freedom. By national freedom we mean freedom from White domination and the attainment of political independence. This implies the rejection of the conception of segregation, apartheid, trusteeship, or White leadership, which are all in one way or another motivated by the idea of White domination or domination of the Whites over the Blacks. Like all other people the African people claim the right of self-determination."

In regard to methods of achieving its objects it makes provision for the following:-

> "2(c) The regular issue of propaganda material through:-
>
> 1. The usual press, newsletter or other means of disseminating our ideas in order to raise the standard of political and national consciousness.
>
> 2. Establishment of a national press.
>
> 3(a) ....to employ the following weapons:-
>
> immediate and active boycott, strike, civil disobedience, non-co-operation and such other means as may bring about the accomplishment and realization of our aspirations.
>
> (b) Preparations and making of plans for a national stoppage of work for one day as a mark of protest against the reactionary policy of the Government."

4. The evidence shows with reference to the methods set out in the Programme of Action that:-

   (i) The successful outcome of these methods depended on the non-European masses presenting an organised and united front to coerce the Government or the electorate through mass actions.

   (ii) That the African National Congress in its endeavour to raise the political consciousness of the masses caused to be published a bulletin called "Congress Voice." In addition it encouraged its volunteers and members to read and support other publications such as "The African Lodestar," "Afrika," "New Age," "Fighting Talk," and a number of other publications all containing propagandist material.

   (iii) That the methods set out in paragraph 3(a) of the Programme of Action envisaged the use of illegal means.

With reference to the illegality of these methods Luthuli, the President General of the African National Congress, said during the course of his evidence

1. That the application of the methods laid down could, with reference to "strike" action when used as a political action, lead in certain circumstances to a direct clash between the African people, the working class on the one hand and the ruling class on the other.

2. That in the breaking of the laws of the land, the State, in pursuance of its duties to maintain law and order, as it saw the position, might be forced to adopt certain measures such as calling out the forces.

He added, however, that in the event of violence and bloodshed ensuing, the African National Congress would not regard or visualize such violence or bloodshed as emanating from it "because the African National Congress would carry on its struggle on a non-violent basis, even in the face of a clash, if there should be one. It would in such event not be a clash of the African National Congress."

5. With reference to the propagandist material used or recommended by the African National Congress and the other organisations for consumption by their members, the systems of Government in the Western Democracies such as the United States of America, the United Kingdom and also South Africa, were condemned and were described as belonging to the war-mongering, imperialistic and oppressor camps, whilst the Eastern Democracies such as Soviet Russia and the Chinese Republic and others received admiration and adulation, and were described as belonging to the peace and freedom loving camps.

Apart from such material, the leaders of the Congress Alliance verbally endorsed such views at various meetings.

6. With reference to the Defiance Campaign against what was termed "Unjust Laws" launched by the African National Congress and the South African Indian Congress in 1952, the outcome thereof was the prosecution and imprisonment of some 8,000 people who were persuaded by these organisations to break certain laws. In the case of the 1954/1955 Western Areas Campaign, directed at preventing the Government from removing the inhabitants from Sophiatown and environs to Meadowlands, the National Executive Committee of the African National Congress claimed that the Government was obliged to declare a state of emergency in the affected areas for a period of three weeks as a result of the campaigning of the African National Congress, and that the presence of about 2,000 Police was required whilst the initial removal of some 150 families was being undertaken.

7. Notwithstanding the above, and the further campaigns, namely, the Anti-Pass Campaign and the campaign against the Bantu Education Act, and the Campaign for the Congress of the People, no violence ensued. In fact, in its Further Particulars the Crown made it clear that it was not alleged that violence resulted from the activities of the various organisations.

8(a) The Crown, in order to prove the violent policy of the Congress Alliance, laid before the Court innumerable documents and reports of speeches held at hundreds of meetings, all in support of the Liberatory Movement. The documents in the main consisted of:-

1. Official reports and minutes of different organisations.
2. Official publications of these organisations.
3. Documents of which leaders of the organisations were the authors.
4. Literature such as bulletins and magazines published by well-disposed persons or bodies, and which the Congress Alliance recommended its members to read.

(b) The speeches, of which reports were produced, were made mainly in Johannesburg, and its environs, in the Port Elizabeth area, in Cape Town, and a few in the Eastern Transvaal. The number of speeches on which the Crown relies represents a minute percentage of the total number of speeches made during the indicted period of four years, and the Court is uninformed as to the nature of the majority of speeches so delivered. The reports of the speeches, with some exceptions, were made by officials who took them down in longhand, and only a small selected percentage of what was said at such meetings was recorded, and in general these reports are open to grave criticism.

(c) In so far as a number of official documents of the African National Congress is concerned, the African National Congress stated that its policy was non-violence, consonant with what was said by many speakers at various meetings.

9. The general trend of speeches made by various members of the African National Congress and of the other organisations, the propaganda and other documentary material relied upon, was to lay stress upon the importance of presenting a united front against the "fascist" Government and its "oppressive" laws, coupled with repeated warnings that the Government would harden and become more "brutal," not hesitating to create a "blood bath" as the liberatory struggle progressed. The people were warned that in the struggle many hardships would have to be endured, and that they might have to pay with their blood and even to make "the supreme sacrifice" to gain freedom. Constant references were made to the struggles of "oppressed" people against imperialist oppressors in other parts of the world such as Korea, Kenya, India and elsewhere, and the people were told that final victory would eventually come to the struggling masses. During the course of these various campaigns, some of the leaders of the African National Congress made themselves guilty of sporadic speeches of violence, which in our opinion amounted to an incitement to violence, but having regard to the total number of speeches made, these form an insignificant part thereof.

10. With reference to the Freedom Volunteers the indictment alleges that the objects would be achieved inter alia by:-

"4(b)ii. Recruiting, enlisting and preparing for acts of violence a special corps of Freedom Volunteers."

The accused Resha, then the Volunteer in Chief for the Transvaal, admittedly in addressing a meeting of African National Congress delegates on the 22nd November, 1956, in Johannesburg, inter alia said:-

SELECTED DOCUMENTS

75

"When you are disciplined and you are told by the organisation not to be violent, you must not be violent. If you are a true volunteer and are called upon to be violent, you must be absolutely violent, and you must murder, murder."

The replay of the tape recording of this speech revealed that there was a thunderous applause from the assembled delegates immediately after Resha had concluded this sentence.

On the other hand the trend of many speeches made by various leaders of the African National Congress and also the documentary evidence, reveal that volunteers were required to carry out the policy of the African National Congress, to be disciplined and not to become violent even in the face of provocation.

It is impossible therefore for the Court to find that the above allegations in the indictment have been proved by the Prosecution.

11. On all the evidence presented to this Court and on our findings of fact, it is impossible for this Court to come to the conclusion that the African National Congress had acquired or adopted a policy to overthrow the State by violence, i.e. in the sense that the masses had to be prepared or conditioned to commit direct acts of violence against the State.

12. Mr. Trengove, on behalf of the Prosecution, however, presented a further argument based on all the evidence, but with special reference to the Programme of Action, and which proceeded on the following lines:-

The African National Congress realised that their struggle and illegal methods employed would bring them into conflict with the State, and they realised that it would lead to a violent clash, at least from the side of the State. He submitted that the African National Congress, by constantly condemning the system in this country on the one hand, and on the other hand praising the systems in the "other camps," indicated a powerful desire or fostering of a mental attitude which would not baulk at the overthrow of this Government, or any other violent action directed towards the downfall of the State as presently constituted. He added that if with such a programme and a state of mind, the African National Congress deliberately provoked the Government into taking measures to maintain law, it was not only responsible for the consequences, but that the African National Congress also intended violence and bloodshed through the application of their illegal methods in order to achieve their freedom. He explained the essence of the Crown case was not only that the African National Congress expected violence from the State, but that it also intended the masses actively to retaliate.

13. We have set out Counsel's argument in some detail because it has to be analysed in the light of the allegations contained in the indictment, the evidence as a whole, and the general probabilities. In so far as the indictment as read with the Further Particulars is concerned, we are of the opinion:-

(i) That although the means whereby the conspirators planned to overthrow the State by violence were set out in the indictment and were elucidated in the Further Particulars, nowhere was it alleged specifically that the conspirators planned to provoke and compel the State, by means of the application of methods under the Programme of Action, to resort to the use of force as a result whereof the masses would retaliate and so bring about the violent overthrow of the State.

(ii) We do not think that it was the intention of the Prosecution to rely on any such plan. If this had been the case, we would have expected some reference in the indictment, or at least in the Further Particulars, to the Programme of Action, and at the very least, proof forthcoming from the Crown of the existence of such a Programme of Action, a matter which was proved by the Defence and not by the Crown.

14. In any event, on the facts we find that though Defence witnesses have stated that they foresaw the possibility of the State being compelled to use violence in certain contingencies, there is insufficient evidence to find that the African National Congress had adopted a plan which revealed a general expectation of violence by the State and an intention to use the masses in retaliation.

15. Whilst therefore the Prosecution has succeeded in showing that the Programme of Action contemplated the use of illegal methods, and that its application in fact resulted in illegal action during the Defiance Campaign, and that the African National Congress, as a matter of policy, decided to employ such means for the achievement of a fundamentally different State from the present, it has failed to show that the African National Congress as a matter of policy intended to achieve this new State by violent means.

The accused are accordingly found not guilty and are discharged.

V. INDEXES

Numbering of Pages by Date, Volume, and Reel

Date	Page	Volume (with 1st page)	Reel
Aug. 3, 1959	1	1 (1)	1
4	117		
5	143	2 (201)	
6	252		
7	376		
		3 (401)	
10	453		
11	564		
		4 (601)	2
12	691		
		5 (801)	
13	812		
14	940		
		6 (1001)	
17	1003		
18	1115		
		7 (1201)	3
19	1236		
20	1343		
		8 (1401)	
21	1449		
24	1492		
25	1584		
		9 (1601)	
26	1691		
27	1791		
		10 (1801)	
28	1930		

Date	Page	Volume (with 1st page)	Reel
Aug. 31, 1959	1995		
		11 (2001)	4
Sept. 1, 1959	2102		
		12 (2201)	
2	2230		
3	2343		
		13 (2401)	
4	2445		
8	2478		
9	2585		
		14 (2601)	5
10	2668		
11	2777		
		15 (2801)	
14	2838		
15	2941		
		16 (3001)	
16	3053		
17	3160(a)		
		17 (3201)	6
18	3243		
21	3320		
		18 (3401)	
22	3414		
23	3539		
		19 (3601)	
24	3648		
25	3740		
28	3794		
		20 (3801)	
29	3872		
30	3979		
		21 (4001)	7
Oct. 1, 1959	4088		

INDEXES 79

Date	Page	Volume (with 1st page)	Reel
Oct. 6, 1959	4132		
		22 (4201)	
7	4218		
8	4309		
9	4397		
		23 (4401)	8
12	4444		
		24 (4601)	
13	4515		
14	4579		
15	4614		
16	4711		
19	4772		
		25 (4801)	
20	4882		
21	4983		
		26 (5001)	9
22	5097		
26	5175(a)		
		27 (5201)	
27	5271		
28	5358		
		28 (5401)	
Nov. 2, 1959	5461		
3	5566		
		29 (5601)	
4	5664		
5	5777		
		30 (5801)	
6	5892		
9	5951		
		31 (6001)	10
10	6051		
11	6171		
		32 (6201)	

Date	Page	Volume (with 1st page)	Reel
Nov. 12, 1959	6291		
17	6401	33 (6401)	
18	6565		
		34 (6601)	11
19	6681		
23	6787		
		35 (6801)	
24	6872		
	[Exhibits: 6879-7396]		
		36 (7001)	
		37 (7201)	
Jan. 18, 1960	7401	38 (7401)	
19	7532		
		39 (7601)	12
20	7669		
21	7764		
		40 (7801)	
22	7876		
25	7921		
		41 (8001)	
26	8026		
27	8129		
28	8192		
		42 (8201)	13
29	8287		
Feb. 1, 1960	8327		
		43 (8401)	
2	8417		
3	8509		
4	8696		
		44 (8701)	
5	8807		
8	8836		
		45 (8901)	

Date	Page	Volume (with 1st page)	Reel
Feb. 9, 1960	8922		
10	9005		
		46 (9101)	14
11	9112		
15	9246		
		47 (9301)	
16	9340		
17	9417		
18	9496		
		48 (9501)	
22	9553		
23	9636		
		49 (9701)	
24	9755		
25	9856		
		50 (9901)	
26	9952		
29	10009		
		51 (10101)	15
March 1, 1960	10103		
2	10183		
		52 (10301)	
3	10329		
4	10419		
7	10467		
		53 (10501)	
8	10578		
9	10673		
		54 (10701)	16
10	10772		
14	10851		
		55 (10900)	
15	10939		
16	11045		
		56 (11101)	17

Date	Page	Volume (with 1st page)	Reel
March 17, 1960	11155		
18	11259		
		57 (11301)	
21	11328		
22	11444		
		58 (11501)	
23	11552		
24	11647		
		59 (11701)	
25	11746		
28	11799		
29	11891		
		60 (11901)	
30	11979		
31	11995		
April 1, 1960	12012		
19	12046		
26	12084		

Note: Page 12099 is followed by page 13000.

		61 (13001)	18
27	13022		
28	13053		
29	13081		
May 2, 1960	13111		
3	13165		
		62 (13201)	
4	13223		
5	13258		
6	13308		
9	13341		
10	13372		
		63 (13401)	
11	13414		
12	13452		

INDEXES   83

Date	Page	Volume (with 1st page)	Reel
May 13, 1960	13513		
16	13551		
17	13591		
		64 (13601)	
18	13641		
19	13671		
20	13709		
24	13750		
25	13801	65 (13801)	
June 1, 1960	13831		
2	13875		
3	13943		
6	13991		
		66 (14001)	19
7	14061		
8	14155		
		67 (14201)	
9	14230		
10	14321		
13	14367		
		68 (14401)	
14	14432		
15	14464		
16	14575		
		69 (14601)	20
17	14680		
20	14744		
		70 (14801)	
21	14834		
22	14915		
23	14990		
		71 (15001)	
24	15101		
27	15172		

Date	Page	Volume (with 1st page)	Reel
		72 (15201)	
June 28, 1960	15235		
29	15323		
		73 (15401)	
30	15426		
July 18, 1960	15501		
26	15579		
Aug. 1, 1960	15585		
		74 (15601)	21
2	15658		
3	15737(a)		
4	15798		
		75 (15801)	
5	15871		
8	15940		
		76 (16001)	
9	16026		
15	16027		
16	16096		
		77 (16201)	22
17	16206		
18	16300		
19	16396		
		78 (16401)	
22	16471		
23	16591		
		79 (16601)	
24	16630		
29	16742		
		80 (16801)	
30	16828		
31	16928		
Sept. 1, 1960	16981		
		81 (17001)	23
6	17119		

INDEXES   85

Date	Page	Volume (with 1st page)	Reel
		82(17201)	
Sept. 7, 1960	17217		
8	17322		
19	17355		
		83 (17401)	
20	17425		
21	17521		
		84(17601)	
22	17621		
23	17731		
27	17767		
		85 (17801)	
Oct. 3, 1960	17823		
4	17931		
		86(18001)	24
5	18016		
6	18108		
		87(18201)	
7	18209		

(Note: The last page of reel 24 is 18322.)

Reel 25 of the Hoover Institution's microfilm is not part of the main treason trial record. It contains the Court's "Reasons for Judgment" (Mr. Justice Rumpff, 168 pages; Mr. Justice Kennedy, 88 pages; Mr. Justice Bekker, 169 pages), preceded by the nineteen schedules accompanying the opinions. Schedule No. 1 is the judgment of March 29, 1961. Schedule No. 2 is the second indictment. Schedule No. 3 is the Prosecution's Summary of Facts. Schedule No. 4 is the admissions of fact made by the Defense. Schedules numbered 5, 7-9, 12-15, and 19 are documents that are included in the List of Selected Documents, below. The remaining schedules include a 36-page summary of evidence by the Prosecution's expert witness on communism (Schedule No. 6) and excerpts from Fighting Talk, Liberation, Advance, New Age, and African Lodestar.

List of Selected Documents

Note: The Prosecution was prepared under the first indictment to offer about 9,000 documents in evidence. This number was reduced to some 4,000 to 5,000 documents under the second indictment.

The short list of forty-one documents below is limited mainly to formal documents that set forth an organization's policies or report on its activities. Some documents, particularly those under the last subheading, are listed because of the importance ascribed to them by the Prosecution. Many are abridged. (The schedules referred to below are in reel 25 of the microfilm. The other pages listed are in reels 1-24.)

For an organizational guide to the documents, see Index of Documents by Organization or Person, below.

African National Congress (national)

Constitution of 1912 [extracts]	3557-3558, 17934
Constitution of the African National Congress, adopted December 16, 1943	Schedule No. 5, pp. 1-10
Africans' Claims in South Africa (booklet). Includes Preface by Dr. A.B. Xuma, president general of the African National Congress, 10716-10719; The Atlantic Charter from the standpoint of Africans within the Union of South Africa, 10723-10730; "Bill of Rights," 10731-10738; List of Members of the Committee, 10738-10740. The findings were adopted by the Annual Conference of the African National Congress, December 16, 1945.	10716-10740
Programme of Action, adopted December 1949 at Annual Conference	10878-10880
Presidential address by Albert J. Luthuli at the Annual Conference, December 1953	Schedule No. 12, pp. 1-6
Presidential address by Albert J. Luthuli at the Annual Conference, December 19, 1954	Schedule No. 14, pp. 8-13
Resolutions of the Annual Conference, 1954	183-187
National Executive Committee, Annual Report to the Annual Conference, December 16-19, 1954	Schedule No. 14, pp. 13-32 (also see 234-251, 257-292)

INDEXES 87

    National Executive Committee, Annual Report to the Annual Conference, December 16-18, 1955 — 3355-3361

    "Basic Policy of the African National Congress Youth League" — 10865-10866

African National Congress (Cape)

    Annual Conference Report, [no date] 1952 — 3860-3865

    Annual Conference Report, June 18-19, 1955 (translated from a Bantu language) — 211-223

    Presidential address by Professor Z.K. Matthews at the Provincial Conference, August 15, 1953 — 18264-18276

    Presidential address by Professor Z.K. Matthews at the Provincial Conference, June 1954 — 18277-18284

    Presidential address by Professor Z.K. Matthews at the Provincial Conference, June 18-19, 1955 — 18285-18307

African National Congress (Natal)

    Annual Executive Report, [no date] 1954 — 225-231

    Report of Provincial Executive Committee for October 1, 1955, to June 30, 1956 — 10847M-10847HH

    Presidential address by Albert J. Luthuli (provincial president), July 26, 1956 — 10847A-10847L

African National Congress (Transvaal)

    Executive Committee, Minutes, February 20, 1955 — 343-344

    Presidential address ("No Easy Walk to Freedom") by Nelson R. Mandela, read for him at the Annual Provincial Conference, September 21, 1953 — Schedule No. 13, pp. 1-17

    Presidential address by E.P. Moretsele at the Provincial Conference, 1954 — Schedule No. 15, pp. 1-4

    Presidential address by E.P. Moretsele at the Provincial Conference; opening address by Dr. H.M. Moosa, vice-president of the Transvaal Indian Congress; November 3-4, 1956 — 1334-1337, 1349-1352

South African Indian Congress

21st Annual Conference, July 9-11, 1954 [no title] — 436-452, 522-560, 581-626

Presidential address by Dr. G.M. Naicker at the Annual Conference, October 19, 1956 — 1438-1442

Natal Indian Congress

Agenda Book, Annual Conference, 1948 — 3767-3769

Agenda Book, Provincial Conference, February 5-7, 1954 — 2561-2580, 2585-2588

Agenda Book, Provincial Conference, March 25-27, 1955 — 401-436

Address by Dr. G.M. Naicker, President of the Natal Indian Congress, delivered at the Annual Conference of the African National Congress, December 19, 1954 — Schedule No. 14, pp. 2-8

South African Congress of Democrats

Constitution [excerpts; no date] — 1522-1524

Chairman's Report to the First Annual Conference; resolutions adopted; June 24, 1955 — 1527-1533, 1537-1542

Congress of the People

Report of the Joint Planning Council of the African National Congress and the South African Indian Congress, by J.S. Moroka, J.B. Marks, W.M. Sisulu, Y.M. Dadoo, and Y. Cachalia, November 8, 1951 — 14992-15003

Freedom Charter, adopted June 25-26, 1955 — Schedule No. 7, pp. 1-5 (also 157-162)

"The Struggle against Passes," Report of the National Consultative Committee to the Joint Executives of the A.N.C., S.A.I.C., S.A.C.P.O, S.A.C.O.D., and the S.A.C.T.U. [included in the Report of the African National Congress Conference of 1956] — Schedule No. 19, pp. 1-5 (also 1450-1454)

INDEXES

Miscellaneous Communist and Left-Wing Documents

Central Committee of the Communist Party of South Africa; extracts from statements issued June 22, 1941 – December 1942	7080-7082
Central Committee of the Communist Party of South Africa, Resolution, "Dissolution of the C.P. of S.A.," June 24, 1950	3113-3114
South Africans in the Soviet Union (printed booklet)	829-833
Report of the South African Delegation to the Third World Youth Congress (typewritten, no date)	2842-2847, 10772
Economics and Politics in South Africa (printed, not dated, unsigned; described by the Prosecution as of considerable importance)	2542-2559
Three lectures ("The World We Live In," "The Country We Live In," and "Change Is Needed") probably written by Lionel Bernstein of the South African Congress of Democrats	Schedule No. 9, pp. 1-40 (also 626-640b, 645-668)
Joseph Slovo, "The Congress of the People," in Liberation, No. 10, 1954	162-168
Nelson R. Mandela, "In Our Lifetime," in Liberation, No. 19, June 1956	Schedule No. 8, pp. 1-6 (also 3539-3545)

List of Selected Transcripts of Meetings

Note: The Prosecution's evidence covered some 280 meetings and two to eight speeches at each meeting, according to the Chief Judge (page 16744). Sometimes more than eight speeches were delivered. According to the Defense in February 1959, the Prosecution had reduced the number of meetings on which evidence would be offered from 504 under the first indictment to 486 under the second; the number of speeches had been reduced to 1,742 from a much larger number. Mr. Justice Bekker pointed out in his reasons for judgment (page 44) that the Prosecution "relied in the nett result on alleged violent utterances made by some, but not all the speakers, at 85 meetings out of a total of some 15,000 meetings which were held by the organisation during the period of the indictment." No independent calculation has been made for the present guide.

Forty-two meetings are listed below because they are important or typical or because the transcript is lengthy. All the listed meetings were recorded either by shorthand or on tape. Meetings recorded by longhand are not included. The list does not, of course, include all meetings that may be considered important.

The transcripts in nearly every case record only portions of meetings, but some of these portions cover several hours of speechmaking, interjections, songs, the reading of messages, and so on. The same meeting may be described or its transcript read at different places in the record. More than one witness may testify to the same meeting. Additional portions of a transcript may be read into the record during cross-examination by the Defense, or two transcripts of the same meeting may be compared by the Defense. The page references also include pages on which the witness is being asked about the circumstances in which a meeting was held or the circumstances in which he recorded the meeting.

For a fuller guide to the meetings, see the Index of Names, below.

African National Congress

January 30, 1955; Sophiatown, Johannesburg	7485-7502, 7945-7947, 7751-7759, 7969-7972
June 9, 1955; Sophiatown, Johannesburg	7469-7484
August 28, 1955; Moroka, Johannesburg	7724-7751, 7552-7556, 7761-7762, 7950-7956
April 29, 1956; Newclare, Johannesburg	7634-7644

INDEXES 91

    April 29, 1956; Sophiatown, Johannesburg   7816-7832
        Note: ANC Youth League meeting.

    June 3, 1956; Moroka, Johannesburg   7644-7652

    June 26, 1956; Cape Town   8079-8081, 8092

    November 22, 1956; meeting at 37 West Street, Johannesburg   8124 ff.; transcript on 8141-8162 (Resha speech begins on 8149); translation of speeches delivered in a Bantu language, 8163-8167, 8167-8178
        Note: Secretly tape-recorded.

    December 9, 1956 (after the treason arrests); Sophiatown, Johannesburg; meeting by "People's Defence Committee"   7663-7670

South African Indian Congress

    July 9, 1954; Durban; National Conference   7987-7990

Natal Indian Congress

    March 25-26, 1955; Durban; Annual Conference   7996-8003, 8039-8041

    June 22, 1956; Durban; Annual Conference   8011-8014, 8047-8049

South African Congress of Democrats

    September 8, 1953; Johannesburg   7913-7919, 10809-10814
        Note: Meeting with the Springbok Legion.

    December 1, 1955; Johannesburg   7618-7628

    February 25, 1956; Johannesburg   7964-7968
        Note: Farewell meeting for Father Huddleston.

    March 2, 1956; Johannesburg   7964-7967

South African Congress of Trade Unions

    January 8, 1956; Johannesburg   7960-7961
        Note: Meeting called to protest against closing of Soviet Consulate.

    February 8, 1956; Johannesburg   7628-7633

February 12, 1956; Durban	8008-8011, 8045-8047
March 4, 1956; Cape Town	8069-8074, 8083-8087
April 22, 1956; Johannesburg	7804-7816, 7883-7885, 7894-7895, 7898, 7906-7911
September 23, 1956; Kliptown, Johannesburg	7866-7874, 7890, 7894, 7898, 7911-7912

South African Coloured People's Organisation

March 13, 1956; Cape Town Note: Page 8074 in error describes meeting as sponsored by S.A.C.T.U.	8074-8077, 8087

Federation of South African Women

May 29, 1955; Johannesburg	7792, 7797-7804, 7882-7883, 7898
August 7, 1955; Johannesburg Note: "Congress of Mothers."	7528-7552

Joint Meetings

May 1, 1954; Cape Town; United May Day Committee meeting	8057-8063
June 27, 1954; Johannesburg; Resist Apartheid Conference	7406-7431, 7767-7777, 7940-7945
July 11, 1954; "Western Areas," Johannesburg; Resist Apartheid Conference, speech by Albert J. Luthuli	11522-11525
July 25, 1954; Johannesburg; meeting sponsored by A.N.C., S.A.C.P.O., T.I.C., and S.A.C.O.D.	7432-7448, 7452-7469
March 20, 1955; Sophiatown, Johannesburg; Colonial Youth Day Rally	7503-7528, 7947-7948
December 11, 1955; Durban; meeting sponsored by A.N.C., N.I.C., and S.A.C.O.D.	8006-8008, 8042-8045, 8063-8069, 8081-8083, 8095-8096

Congress of the People

September 8, 1954; Durban; speech by Dr. G.M. Naicker at first Natal Conference of C.O.P.	2043-2050

INDEXES

December 5, 1954; Pietermaritzburg; meeting of Midlands Region C.O.P.	8017-8039
May 21, 1955; Johannesburg; meeting of Transvaal C.O.P.	7778-7792, 7880-7882, 7894, 7898
June 12, 1955; Durban; meeting of the Natal Action Council of C.O.P.	8004-8006, 8040-8042
June 25-26, 1955; Kliptown, Johannesburg; first national meeting of the Congress of the People	6486-6526 (reprinted 10270-10316; see also 7878-7880, 10261-10263, 10317 ff.)
September 18, 1955; Johannesburg; meeting of Freedom Charter Committee	7566-7599, 7972-7973
June 24, 1956; Kliptown, Johannesburg; first anniversary meeting of the Congress of the People	7833-7866, 7885-7890, 7895, 7900-7906

South African Society for Peace and Friendship with the U.S.S.R.

February 9, 1954; Johannesburg	7921-7930
November 7, 1954; Johannesburg	7930-7939
November 6, 1955; Johannesburg	7599-7618, 7956-7960
November 7, 1956; Johannesburg	7652-7663, 7961-7964

Index of Documents by Organization or Person

Note: The 4,000 to 5,000 documents submitted as evidence by the Prosecution included printed books and pamphlets, magazines and newspapers, mimeographed reports, bulletins and circulars, typewritten and handwritten documents, and a miscellaneous assortment of flyers, memoranda, and official and personal letters. These were found in offices and homes and at meetings, on open tables, in bookcases, in desks and briefcases, and in the possession of individuals during more than a thousand searches and raids.

For the most part, the record includes only the portions of documents that were read in court. Some documents that were read in part were later inserted into the record in full without being read. Some documents appear in the record only by their title or by a brief description. Others were referred to on many occasions in order to indicate that they had been in the possession of one of the accused.

The Prosecution concluded the submission of nearly all its documents on October 14, 1959. A few more were introduced later, and the Defense also introduced some documents. The index below is limited to the record for the period of August 3, 1959, through October 14, 1959.

The index is limited also to documents represented in the record by at least a substantial paragraph and to documents that can be attributed to an organization or to an individual. Documents are attributed to individuals only if they cannot be attributed to an organization. Reference is made only to the page on which an extract from a document, or a complete document, begins.

Africa Committee of the Communist Party, London, 2944

African Laundry, Cleaning and Dyeing Workers Union, 3338, 3339, 3342, 3343, 3344, 3345, 3346, 3347

African National Congress, 144, 175, 884, 925, 927, 928, 929, 984, 992, 996, 1051, 1052, 1368, 1437, 1471, 1485, 1584, 1663, 1861, 1985, 2034, 2057, 2066, 2067, 2069, 2077, 2128, 2211, 2225, 2422, 2613, 2630, 2631, 2633, 2641, 2772, 2778, 2779, 2794, 2808, 2810, 2859, 2918, 2920, 3093, 3098, 3114, 3120, 3160(g), 3160(i), 3160(j), 3164, 3165, 3166, 3172, 3178, 3179, 3187, 3189, 3217, 3222, 3226, 3331, 3355, 3372, 3379, 3385, 3395, 3411, 3424, 3433, 3455, 3557, 3562, 3778, 3779, 3798, 3833, 3834, 3842, 3860, 4021, 4208, 4212, 4250, 4329, 4336, 4337, 4341, 4343, 4344, 4352, 4360(a), 4414, 4446, 4464, 4470, 4491, 4594, 4596, 4601

———— Alexandra Branch, 2637, 3094

———— Bloemfontein Branch, 3119

———— Cape Provincial Branch, 198, 200, 211, 879, 1014, 2772, 3160(k), 3164, 3166, 3210, 3430, 3783, 3819,

INDEXES 95

3848, 3860, 3875, 3878, 4144, 4315, 4448, 4466

———— Cape Western Branch, 4497

———— Durban Branch, 4200

———— Eastern Cape Regional Committee, 3813, 3873

———— Germiston Branch, 3183

———— Jabavu Branch, 4320

———— Kimberley Branch, 2284

———— Natal Provincial Branch, 225, 984, 1052, 2777, 2778, 2831, 3165, 3390, 3412, 3427, 3445, 3702, 3709, 4160, 4174, 4182, 4251, 4281, 4283

———— National Executive Committee, 234, 257, 1028, 1152, 1407, 2057, 2299, 2787, 2816, 2819, 2885, 3113, 3417, 3452, 3453, 3556, 3566, 3785, 3792, 3834, 4207, 4338, 4345, 4435, 4457

———— New Brighton Branch, 3803, 3815, 3850, 3997, 3998

———— Orange Free State Provincial Branch, 4327, 4344

———— Sophiatown Branch, 3141

———— ———— Working Committee, 4135

———— Southwestern Region, 3235

———— Transvaal Provincial Branch, 343, 1300, 1635, 1666, 2065, 2066, 2178, 2530, 2533, 2640, 2908, 3099, 3154, 3160(b), 3160(f), 3180, 3223, 3372, 3411, 3555, 4306, 4383

———— ———— Executive Committee, 3085, 3121, 3175

———— Western Region, 2068, 4581

———— Working Committee, 3787

African National Congress Women's League, 1316, 1369, 2636, 2777, 3160(j), 3209, 4324, 4325, 4328, 4333, 4334, 4335, 4340, 4342, 4344, 4346, 4363, 4385

———— Bloemfontein Branch, 4367

———— Cape Provincial Branch, 4327

———— National Executive Committee, 4339

———— Transvaal Provincial Branch, 2826, 4387

African National Congress Youth League, 148, 1022, 1024, 1051, 1146, 1261, 2611, 2634, 2815, 3077, 3112, 3147, 3156, 3374, 3812, 3851, 3989, 3997, 4134, 4247, 4249, 4325

———— Cape Provincial Branch, 4267, 4317, 4355

———— New Brighton Branch, 3823, 3984, 4273

———— Orlando Branch, 4260

———— Summer School, 3714

———— Transvaal Provincial Branch, 841, 850, 872, 946, 1307, 1981, 1998, 2580, 2944, 2945, 3126, 3133, 3138, 3144, 3160(a), 3170, 3182, 3262, 3414, 3432

Alliance of the Liberatory and Trade Union Movements, 2965

All-In African Conference (African Ministers' Federation), 3213

Area Council, 4542

Basutoland African Congress, 2589

Bernstein, Lionel (Rusty), 2446

Cape Town Peace Conference, 2737

Cape Town Peace Council, 1869, 1870, 1916, 2005, 2006, 2224, 2232, 2244, 2245, 4526, 4580

Cape Town Regional Peace Convention, 2737

Colonial Youth Day (organized by the ANCYL Transvaal, TIYC, COD Youth Section, and SACPO Youth Section), 1304, 1872, 2821, 3803, 3995, 4261

Colonial Youth Week, 2830

Communist Party of South Africa, 3108, 3109, 3113

Competent Publishing and Printing Pty., Ltd., 2228

Conco, Dr. W.Z., 3672

Conference Committee of the ANC Transvaal, TIC, SACOD, and SACPO, 202

Congress of the People, 156, 162, 773, 902, 934, 1034, 1051, 1052, 1153, 1181, 1185, 1194, 1198, 1215, 1256, 1268, 1278, 1304, 1375, 1427, 1449, 1587, 1591, 2038, 2283, 2352, 2497, 2513, 2656, 2684, 2686, 2687, 3092, 3208, 3985, 4006, 4013, 4136, 4138, 4150, 4371, 4519, 4593, 4598

———— Cape Eastern Provincial Committee of the National Action Council, 3802, 3984

———— Cape Sponsoring Organisations, 3800

———— Cape Western Action Council, 2679, 2680, 2692

———— Eastern Cape Region Action Committee, 2683, 3983, 3985

———— Johannesburg Regional Committee, 1206, 1213, 1217, 1219, 2128, 2130, 2287, 2304

———— Korsten Action Committee, 3807

———— Natal Action Committee, 1591, 2493, 2495, 2681, 3664, 3668, 3671, 3797, 3839, 4215

———— Natal Congress of the People Conference, 2022, 3668

———— Natal Midlands Region, 2678, 2691, 2692, 4169

———— National Action Council, 883, 944, 1206, 1222, 1587, 1675, 2058, 2232, 2237, 2287, 2294, 2681, 2682, 2683, 2686, 2687, 2688, 2689, 2726, 3660, 3661, 3662, 3665, 3668, 3671, 3776, 3777, 3793, 3795, 3798, 3985, 3986, 4471, 4486, 4537

———— New Brighton (Port Elizabeth) Action Committee, 3833

———— Provincial Committee, 2303

———— South African Action Council, 2689

———— Transvaal Action Council, 1203, 1865, 2649

———— Transvaal Provincial Committee, 1204, 1211, 1270, 1591, 2690, 2698, 2699, 2700

———— Transvaal Volunteer Board, 3099

Council of Non-European Trade Unions, 168, 963, 1003

Dhlamini, S., 3713

Durban Peace Council, 1894, 1899

Durban Study Circle, 2461

English Congress of the People, 2022, 2535

Evaton People's Transport Committee, 3079

INDEXES

Federation of South African Women, 1285, 1294, 1300, 1311, 1317, 1366, 1368, 1437, 1508, 1594, 1596, 1934, 1947, 2132, 2383, 2399, 2459, 2502, 2509, 2538, 2539, 2683, 2809, 3165, 3170, 3187, 3218, 3232, 3253, 3321, 4019, 4145, 4330, 4335, 4537

———— National Executive Committee, 2521

———— National Working Committee, 4332

———— Transvaal Regional Executive Committee, 2516, 2524

Fighting Talk Committee, 1407, 1972, 4499

Freedom Charter Consultative Committee, 3812

Freedom Volunteers, 1265, 1592

Friends of the Soviet Union, 1516

Gumede, A., 3672, 4311

Johannesburg Peace Council, 1899

Johannesburg Region Consultative Committee, 3223

Johannesburg Western Areas Anti-Group Areas Joint Committee, 4026, 4121

Joint Action Committee of the ANC and the Natal Indian Congress, 1927

Joint Congress and Legion Committee, 1780

Joint Executive of the ANC, SAIC, SACOD, and SACPO, 1026, 3818

Joint Meeting between the Executive Committee of the Evaton People's Transport Committee and the Directors of the EPS, 2951

Kathrada, A.M., 2583

Kenya Committee for Democratic Rights for Kenya Africans (London), 2220, 2221

Kotane, Moses, 2301

Levy, Leon, 2213, 2214, 2215, 2239, 3369

"Liberation," 2888, 3078, 3458, 3476, 3492, 3495, 3510, 3511, 3521, 3527, 3532, 3534, 3537, 3546, 3547

Luthuli, Albert J., 2236, 2283, 2599, 2602, 2868, 2896, 2968, 3423, 3560, 3705, 3714, 3748, 3817, 3830, 3843, 4249

Makiwane, Tennyson X., 2631

Manana, P.J.S., 3672

Masina, Leslie, 2308, 3333, 3369, 3450

Mass Anti-Removal Conference, 3201

Mathe, J., 2626

Matthews, J.G. (Joe), 3252

Matthews, Professor Z.K., 3668

Mavuso, J.S.A., 2631, 3117

Modern Youth Society, Cape Town, 4499

Molife (Molefi), J.S., 2948

Moolla, E., 3183

Moolla, Moosa, 3779

Motala, M.M. (Dr.), 3665

Mqota (Mgota), T., 4000

Mzo, 2631

Naicker, Dr. G.M., 2249, 2567, 2609, 3729, 3743, 3744, 3746, 3759

Naicker, M.P., 3673

Nair, Billy, 2673, 4186, 4188

Natal Indian Congress, 401, 1107, 1141, 1307, 1470, 1754, 1861, 1928, 1929, 1930, 2043, 2075, 2077, 2079, 2213, 2223, 2496, 2561, 2606, 2831, 3655, 3657, 3658, 3670, 3672, 3674, 3681, 3682, 3694, 3696, 3700, 3701, 3741, 3753, 3767, 4219, 4225, 4235, 4582

Natal Indian Youth Congress, 1314, 1315, 1928, 4173, 4189

Natal Peace Council, 1895, 1920, 2216, 2219, 2246, 2247, 2739, 2931

Natal Provincial Vigilance Committee, 2680

National Action Council of the Congress of the People of the Joint Executive of the ANC, SAIC, SACPO, and SACOD, 1284, 1449, 1480, 1592, 3674

National Consultative Committee of the ANC, SAIC, SACOD, and SACPO, 1216, 1367, 1449, 1481, 1510, 2200, 2605, 3258, 3383, 3412, 4174

National Executive of the ANC, SAIC, SACOD, and SACPO, 3789

National Peace Congress, 1852, 1853, 1854, 1861, 1921, 1958

National Peace Convention Preparatory Committee, 1299, 2736, 2738, 3231

"New Age," 3234, 3259, 3833, 3874, 4541

Ngoyi, Lillian, 2445, 2874

Ngwentshe, A.S., 3883

Nogaya, (B.) A., 4012

Nokwe, P.P. Duma, 2598, 2625

Pan African State Organisation, 4606

Peace Congress Committee, 1861

Pillay, V.S.M., 3672

Pioneer Press, Ltd., 3103

Port Elizabeth Mass People's Conference, 3809

Resha, Robert, 2583, 2656, 4146

Simelane, P.H., 4202, 4309

Sisulu, Walter M., 2562, 2621, 2625, 3826, 3986, 4123, 4262, 4316

Slovo, Ruth (née First), 2239, 2293

South African Coloured People's Organisation, 1152, 1184, 1305, 1313, 1363, 1366, 1437, 1507, 1635, 1640, 1662, 2071, 2380, 2422, 4540, 4543, 4544, 4546, 4547

South African Congress of Democrats, 169, 929, 1033, 1223, 1386, 1456, 1522, 1525, 1526, 1527, 1537, 1543, 1552, 1565, 1566, 1571, 1579, 1580, 1581, 1586, 1590, 1591, 1592, 1633, 1635, 1636, 1643, 1645, 1648, 1653, 1660, 1661, 1665, 1675, 1680, 1687, 1714, 1718, 1738, 1754, 1755, 1781, 1786, 1925, 1926, 1931, 1932, 1997, 2057, 2059, 2060, 2064, 2065, 2074, 2075, 2077, 2083, 2085, 2086, 2087, 2149, 2163, 2166, 2172, 2182, 2184, 2186, 2189, 2218, 2399, 2422, 2431, 2573, 2650, 2718, 2725, 2729, 3356, 3668, 3671, 3798, 3985, 4360, 4407, 4489, 4600

———— Cape Western Region, 2072, 2083

INDEXES

———— Durban Branch, 2206

———— Executive Committee, 1437

South African Congress of Trade Unions, 1309, 1437, 1785, 1990, 2139, 2308, 2317, 2318, 2319, 2321, 2323, 2333, 2430, 3249, 3369, 3370, 3371, 3376, 3393, 3397, 3399, 3402, 3404, 3448, 4298, 4341

———— Management Committee, 3396, 3397, 3402, 3407, 3408

———— National Executive Committee, 3401, 3454

———— Witwatersrand Local Committee, 3371, 3398, 3399, 3403, 3404, 3406

South African Delegation to the Third World Youth Congress, 2842

South African Delegation to the Fourth World Festival of Youth and Students, 2876

South African Indian Congress, 436, 522, 581, 992, 999, 1103, 1107, 1221, 1225, 1321, 1323, 1328, 1386, 1434, 1442, 1454, 1485, 1489, 1929, 2076, 2078, 2422, 2591, 2739, 3067, 3080, 3797, 4142

———— Executive Committee, 2494

South African Indian Youth Congress, 1084, 2573

South African National Peace Convention, 3385, 3408

South African Peace Congress, 1853, 1863, 1902, 2355, 2356, 2400, 2414

South African Peace Council, 912, 914, 917, 920, 923, 1437, 1620, 1628, 1629, 1795, 1797, 1801, 1803, 1804, 1807, 1811, 1830, 1855, 1858, 1859, 1864, 1866, 1867, 1872, 1896, 1897, 1898, 1899, 1901, 1902, 1916, 1918, 1920, 1921, 1922, 1923, 1924, 1932, 1980, 1985, 1987, 2062, 2064, 2073, 2189, 2197, 2212, 2215, 2216, 2217, 2218, 2219, 2220, 2221, 2222, 2223, 2224, 2226, 2227, 2233, 2234, 2236, 2238, 2248, 2249, 2258, 2260, 2345, 2347, 2356, 2372, 2502, 2628, 2744, 2745, 2746, 3185

South African Peace Movement, Provisional Committee, 1895

South African Society for Peace and Friendship with the Soviet Union, 921, 1227, 1306, 1308, 1310, 1313, 1315, 1360, 1456, 1689, 1724, 1996, 2063, 2072, 2197, 2235, 2374, 2391, 2398, 2399, 2435, 2727, 2732, 2751, 2779

Springbok Legion, 1778

Tafali, S., 4326

Tambo, O. (Oliver), 3160

Thompson, Reverend D.C., 2419, 2729

Trade Unions Co-ordinating Committee, 1369, 2286, 2287, 2308, 2317, 2366

Transvaal Consultative Committee of the ANC, SACPO, TIC, SACOD, and SACTU, 145, 1217, 1236, 1352, 1511, 2422, 2528, 3157, 3234, 3257, 3260, 3385, 3388, 4299

Transvaal Council of Non-European Trade Unions, 1635, 2370

Transvaal Indian Congress, 1096, 1116, 1142, 1283, 1305, 1320, 1349, 1635, 1927, 1932

———— Executive Committee, 1143, 1274, 2691, 2698

Transvaal Indian Youth Congress, 1054, 1057, 1072, 1078, 1087, 1090, 1101, 1228, 1256, 1265, 1271, 1283, 1286, 1300, 1315, 1317, 1318, 1319, 1320, 1328, 1330, 1331, 1332, 1333, 1419, 1504, 1505, 1506, 1610, 1700, 1745, 1926, 2215, 2506, 2669, 3185, 4033

Transvaal Peace Conference, 3196, 3214

Transvaal Peace Council, 921, 922, 1308, 1313, 1610, 1633, 1634, 1828, 1864, 1891, 1899, 1923, 1954, 2010, 2249, 2349, 2350, 2370, 2400, 2485, 2486, 2487, 3204, 4145

Transvaal Women's Day (Transvaal Region of the Federation of South African Women), 2611

Tshume, T., 3822, 3833, 3835

Tshunungwa, T.E., 3426, 3672, 3774, 3790, 3791, 3796

Women's International Democratic Federation, 901, 1234, 1843, 1846, 1849

World Federation of Democratic Youth, 890, 898, 919, 1227, 1229, 1295, 1296, 1297, 1681, 1685, 1838, 1841, 3824

World Peace Council, 920, 1295, 1805, 1807, 1808, 1810, 1811, 1825, 1868, 1947, 2061, 2064, 2253, 2254, 2255, 2256, 2257, 2258, 2259, 2735

World Youth Day Committee, 3178

Yengwa, M.B., 3423, 3560, 4198, 4611

Youth Action Committee, 3252

INDEXES

Index of Names

Note: This index of some 380 names is limited mainly to South Africans who have been active in the extraparliamentary opposition. A few sympathizers, among them non-South Africans, are included. About 150 additional persons in this opposition or allied to it are referred to in the microfilm but have not been listed because their activity has been relatively unimportant.

The index includes pages that merely record the fact that a witness knows a certain person. It does not include references to names appearing in extracts from printed magazines and newspapers, for example, Advance and New Age. Nor does it give pages that record a witness's identification of an accused or pages listing names of persons who possessed certain documents.

The record contains frequent variations in the spelling of names, and persons referred to are sometimes difficult to identify. The spelling used below has been decided upon after consultation with some leading members of the opposition. They have also assisted in the effort to identify certain of the persons whose names are misspelled. The index does not, therefore, always correspond with the record or even with the lists that appear in Section III. For example, it follows Lutuli's own preference in the spelling of his name.

Adams, Faried, 517, 1226, 1319, 1320, 1330, 1361, 1376, 1427, 1432, 1460, 1463, 1464, 1465, 1469, 1497, 1499, 1504, 2072, 2360, 2383, 2411, 2492, 3179, 3186, 3252, 3324, 3871, 4174, 4348, 7644, 7647, 8362, 8388, 8448, 8901, 9581-82, 9599, 9601, 13827, 14178, 14631, 15050, 15089, 15230, 15561, 17125

Alexander, Mrs. Ray, 398, 1745, 1845, 1924, 1938, 2137, 2505, 2979, 2999, 3578, 3584, 3596, 3601, 3605, 3638, 4020, 8061-62, 9022, 9067, 13985, 14206-7, 14428, 14811, 16599, 16903

Altman, Mrs. Phyllis, 2930

Amra, Cassim, 423, 525, 527, 3620

Anderson, J., 1582, 3403

Asmal, Mohamed, 2647, 2942, 8224, 8231-32, 8241, 8243-44, 8251, 8258, 8262-63, 8265, 8272, 8278, 8314, 14729, 15083

Asvat, Amina, 7537

Asvat, Dr. Zainab, 15053

Baard, Mrs. Frances, 2148-49, 4339, 4344, 9701, 9708, 9798

Baker, J., 1582, 1782

Baker, Louis, 1528, 1568, 1782, 2085, 2086

Baker, Tumara, 7548

Ballinger, W.G., 8089-90

Baloi, R.G., 11460

Barenblatt, Yetta, 366, 1513, 1514, 1592, 1628, 1642, 1704-5, 1995-97, 2023, 2029, 2035, 2054, 2151, 8389, 14092, 14435, 18198

Barsel, Esther, 1582

Bell, Alex, 4099

Bennie, N.A., 339

Bernstein, Lionel (Rusty), 404, 516, 1208, 1528, 1564, 1653, 1655, 1728, 1782, 1979, 2441, 2442, 2446, 2460, 2470, 2473, 2971, 2987, 2999, 3001, 3002, 3004, 3035, 3633, 3739(D), 3788, 4163, 4350, 4410-11, 4438, 4507, 7917-18, 8325, 8342, 8390, 8419-20, 8556, 11824-25, 13623, 14412, 14435, 14441-42, 14467, 14492, 15097, 15300, 15301, 15304, 15414, 15926, 17121, 17137, 18197

Bernstein, Mrs. Lionel, see Watts, Hilda

Beyleveld, Pieter, 362, 364-65, 470, 689, 767, 943, 1027, 1375, 1566, 1581, 1661, 1782, 2055, 2074, 2076, 2085, 2087-88, 2139, 2149, 2182, 2231, 2284-87, 2290-92, 2297, 2308, 2315, 2422, 2510, 2649, 2725, 2886, 2961, 2984, 3249, 3370, 3394, 3397-98, 3580, 3593, 3665, 3671, 3697, 3786, 3788, 3798, 4007, 4055, 4060, 4061, 4165, 4360(c), 4372, 4447, 7435, 7468, 7601, 7617-18, 7623, 7631, 7670, 7813, 7867, 7914-16, 7989-90, 7993, 7998, 8001, 8062, 8071, 8222, 8350, 8352, 8390, 8425, 8453, 9071, 10951, 11826, 13945, 13980, 13986, 14412-13, 14436, 14438, 14783, 14854, 15414, 15551, 15996

Boikanyo, P.J., 2284

Bokala, Isaac, 8949, 8961, 8997, 9189, 9301, 9320

Bokwe, Dr. R.C., 212, 3790, 4456, 17921, 18261, 18262

Boola, Ismail, 2883, 8518, 10093

Bopape, D.W., 295, 558, 688, 950, 961, 1855, 2699, 2907, 2952, 2953, 3828, 3961, 8776, 8956, 8988, 10090-91, 10100, 13957, 15069, 15772, 16882, 17289, 17811, 18212

Boshielo, Flag, 16065

Boshoff, Advocate Franz, 7918

Bunting, Brian, 398, 829, 1655, 2397, 3029, 3107, 3887, 4515-16, 8431, 9022, 9067, 9346, 9348, 9351-53, 9355, 9439, 13786, 14153, 14428, 14439

Bunting, Mrs. Brian (Sonia), 517, 942, 1375, 1869-70, 1916, 2224, 2233, 2245, 2511, 2984, 3327, 4008, 4120, 4165, 4515-16, 4524-25, 4537, 4567, 4569-70, 8061, 9025, 9342, 9379, 14839

Burford, B.J., 7918

Busakwe, W., 943

Butcher, Mary, 1528

Bux, Raymond, 3653, 3679

Cachalia, Maulvi, 1782, 1852, 1861, 1911, 3935, 4387

Cachalia, Yusuf, 244, 437, 452, 525, 529, 599, 602, 604, 605, 688, 839, 993, 994, 1226, 1434, 1851-52, 1855, 2077, 2224, 2231, 2253, 2356, 2583, 3137, 3593, 3634, 3662, 3788, 3793, 3796, 4448, 8040, 8784, 9135, 9873, 9879, 10084, 11824, 11826, 13420, 14412, 14839-40, 15067, 15073, 15083, 15126, 15128, 15141, 15300, 15414, 16004, 16019, 16022, 16409, 16569, 16570, 16759, 17127, 17787, 17790, 18075, 18216

Calata, Rev. James A., 212, 997, 998, 3849, 3868, 4363, 4599, 11910, 15588, 17638, 17879-80, 17934, 18261, 18262

INDEXES

Carneson, Fred, 404, 519, 3234, 3328, 3330, 3587, 3590, 3599, 3601, 3604-5, 3823, 3833, 3874, 3886, 4120, 4173, 4528, 4565, 4567, 9022, 9067, 9344, 9346, 9350, 9352-53, 9355, 14153, 14428-29, 14439, 14442, 17584, 18197, 18201

Chabanku, June, 8185-86

Chamile, Andries, 7636, 8522, 8948, 8951-52, 8985, 8993, 9319, 9324

Champion, W.A., 11408

Chetty, Dr. B.T., 3768

Choudri, Ashwin, 525

Cohen, Percy, 1860, 3090, 7921, 8321, 8339, 8365, 8696, 14658

Collins, Canon John, 2018, 9149

Conco, H.M., 226, 4575

Conco, Dr. Wilson Z., 225, 231, 274, 275, 276, 326, 345, 361, 763, 925, 942, 943, 1375, 2493, 2774, 2777-78, 3639, 3672-73, 3709, 3789, 3792, 4006, 4038-39, 4145, 4169, 4200, 4213, 4216, 4571-72, 4576, 4577-78, 7439-40, 7945, 8004, 8006, 8013, 8020, 8732, 8809-10, 8815-16, 9046, 9976, 9979, 10851, 10977, 11476, 11813, 11828, 11830, 11835, 11849, 13070, 13260, 13788, 13903-4, 14080, 15635, 16098, 16160, 16256, 16264, 16469, 16475, 16483, 16486, 16581, 16982, 17070, 17398, 17469, 17474, 17500, 17502, 17558, 17577, 17579, 17612, 17740, 17821

Dadoo, Dr. Yusuf M., 266, 437, 451-52, 540, 544, 558, 598, 688, 942, 949, 994, 1057, 1062, 1067, 1091, 1094, 1098, 1284, 1332, 1434, 1854, 1916, 2665, 2952, 2984, 3018, 3068, 3069, 3185-86, 3475, 3591-92, 3597, 3610-11, 3641, 3701, 3760, 3828, 3962, 3977, 4007, 4139, 4279, 4280, 4360(a), 7569, 7849, 7857, 8501-2, 8747, 8776, 8948, 8956, 8988, 9135, 9168, 9617, 9713, 9718, 9756, 9872, 9874, 10090, 10099, 10969, 13304, 13530, 13957, 14980-82, 14995-97, 15005, 15038, 15045, 15049-50, 15068-69, 15071-76, 15082, 15111, 15117, 15119-21, 15130-32, 15214, 15228, 15478, 15777, 15815, 15818, 16017, 16022, 16195-97, 16793-94, 17011-12, 17150, 17429, 17489-90, 18216

Dalindyebo, Chief David, 15759

Damons, Mrs. Stella, 819

Daniels, Adam, 943, 2071, 2422, 4165, 7521, 7523, 7669, 8885, 9336

Davis, Advocate Mike, 15696

Dawood, Miss Assa, 2360

Deane, E.A., 9013, 9015, 9062, 15264, 15266

Desai, Barney, 1062, 2402, 8344, 8762, 8783, 9305, 9469, 16209

Dhlamini, Stephen, 226, 515, 2219, 2422, 3204, 3620, 3668, 3697, 3713, 4070, 4147, 4150, 4161, 4200, 4255, 4256, 7997, 8001, 8009, 8045, 8313, 8720, 8746-47, 8755, 8814, 8816-17, 8820, 10088, 11013, 11014, 11303, 11828, 14838, 15229

Doyle, Alan, 3040

Dube, Dr. John L., 11408

Du Toit, Elizabeth S. (Betty), 3591

Ebrahim, F., 1328

Fazzie, J., 9914

Feinstein, C., 1782, 2991, 2992, 7446, 8344

Festenstein, Mrs., 4516

Fischer, Advocate Abraham (Bram), 1563, 1853-54, 2364, 7918

Fischer, Mrs. Abraham (Molly), 1528, 1782

Fisher, S., 9473, 9477

Fletcher, Melville, 9757, 15260

Forman, Lionel, 518, 1154, 1264, 2148, 2690, 2969, 2942, 2986, 2992, 2997, 2999, 3000, 3063, 3234, 3330, 3587, 3610, 3617, 3631, 3633, 3823, 3849, 4120, 4160, 4173, 4351, 4530-32, 4541, 4569, 8078, 9342, 11392, 11938, 13786, 14153, 14428, 14442, 14476, 14580, 15407, 15847, 15849, 16091-92, 16484, 16647, 17122, 18197

Forsyth, Dr. R., 2930

Friedman, L., 3403, 4360(c), 7808

Fuyani, D., 339, 3851, 3985, 3998, 4273, 9504, 9550-51, 9559, 9651-52, 9739, 9743, 9746, 9994, 15702, 16258

Gangat, I., 527

Gawe, Rev. Walker S., 212, 942, 1014, 2613, 3593, 3816, 3817, 4009, 4315, 4599, 9519, 9521, 9708, 16575, 16576, 17921, 18261, 18262

Gilman, Professor Joseph, 2227, 2264, 2414, 8405

Goldberg, Mrs. Marcelle, 8274, 14241, 14726-27

Goldberg, Victor, 3534

Golding, George, 15263-64

Gomas, J., 15266

Graham, Mrs., 2491

Gumede, Archibald, 225, 1919, 3672-73, 3703, 3792, 4167-72, 4311, 8809, 8814, 8823-24, 10090, 11322, 17533, 17557, 17730

Gwentshe, A.S., 277, 295, 1567

Hadebe, James J., 9957, 9962, 9964, 9967, 10054-55, 10058, 15488, 16903

Harmel, Michael, 1091, 1780, 2486, 2952, 3065, 3137, 3961-62, 4064, 7918, 17137

Hathorn, Dr. Michael, 1782, 8013, 13397

Hauser, George, 11911-12, 11938

Hellman, Dr. Ellen, 17830

Hepner, Mrs. Miriam, 14466

Hepner, Willie, 1582, 8321

Hepple, Alex, 8457-60

Heymann, Issie, 1851, 2489, 7507, 8491, 9239, 14855, 17271-72, 17276

Hlapane, Bartholomew, 3100, 4304, 7556, 7736, 9110, 9859, 17406, 17421, 17425, 17445, 17448-49

Hodgson, Percy John, 404, 467, 517, 1513, 1528, 1572, 1782, 2085, 3102-3, 3160(j), 3327, 3580, 3591, 3725, 3739(D), 4220, 4508, 7407, 8390, 8518, 10085-86, 13974, 14436, 14441, 14467, 14492, 14539, 14542, 15097, 18197

Hodgson, Rica, 1528, 2061, 8362

Hoogendyk, Jan, 2077, 2078, 3661, 3669-70, 10943

Horvitch, Isaac O., 518, 2487, 2909, 2942, 3233, 3330, 3823, 3849, 4173 4508, 4565, 4580, 8057, 9005, 9344 14440, 14442, 18197

Horzuk, A., 9075

INDEXES

Huddleston, Father Trevor, 402, 411-13, 942, 1010, 1473, 2701, 2773, 3686, 3691, 3933, 4007, 4139, 4590, 7409, 7521-22, 7570, 7842, 7849, 7942, 7964-65, 7967, 7997, 8358, 8365, 8367, 8408, 8426, 8519, 8542, 9149, 9234, 9305, 9311, 9756, 9969, 14657, 14658, 14704, 16817, 17844

Hurbans, Gopallal, 365, 452, 525, 942, 1284, 1328, 1375, 2494, 2561, 2736, 3657, 3675-77, 3680, 3695, 3698, 3699, 4007, 4139, 4219, 4237, 4238, 4242, 4243, 4244, 4246, 4591, 8014, 8016, 8709, 8711, 15082

Hutchinson, Alfred, 345, 761, 787, 942, 1304, 1375, 2170, 2701, 2736, 2773, 2810, 2882, 2885, 3025, 3087, 3093, 3164, 3584, 3779, 3835, 3842, 4101, 4139, 4305, 4344, 4355, 4480, 4572, 7568, 7631, 7972, 8344, 8377, 8390, 8419-20, 8560, 9165, 10093, 10977, 11813-14, 13760, 16129, 16303, 16432, 16438, 17173, 17387, 17917-19

Jack, Joseph, 3776, 3799, 3800, 3802, 3803, 3881-82, 9461, 9545, 9621-23, 9633, 9636, 9783, 9785, 9815, 9838, 9903-4, 9913, 9916, 9921, 10044, 15623, 15656, 15702, 15707, 15708, 15718, 15719, 15748, 18040, 18262

Jarrett-Kerr, Father Martin, 1501

Jasson, Christina, 819, 2315, 3985

Jordan, Dr. A.C., 2690, 4160

Joseph, Mrs. Helen, 363-66, 466, 471, 943, 1219, 1294, 1300, 1311, 1317, 1361, 1368, 1369, 1376, 1582, 1752, 1782, 1855, 1856, 1858, 1947, 2136, 2182, 2227-28, 2345, 2356, 2361, 2401, 2411-12, 2501, 2502, 2507, 2508, 2509, 2510, 2512, 2513, 2514, 2520, 2524, 2533, 2535, 2668, 2681, 2683, 2725, 2827, 3025, 3038, 3254-55, 4087, 4165, 4335, 4342, 7546-48, 7607, 7627, 7803, 7854, 8362, 8365, 8389, 8402-3, 8492, 8696, 8885, 9048, 9051, 9967, 11018, 13022, 13124, 13470, 13472-74, 13513-14, 15283, 15332, 15551, 15558, 16505, 16597, 16599, 16606, 16614, 16618, 16621, 16628, 16630, 16649, 16748, 17127, 17427, 17512

Joseph, Paul, 386, 398, 510, 829, 1062, 1125, 1210, 1332, 1432, 1433, 1460, 1463, 1492, 1493, 1496, 1497, 1858, 2084, 2356, 2397, 2407, 2486, 2489, 2662-63, 2753, 2755, 2978, 2999, 3090, 4035, 4453, 7427, 7446, 7607, 7657, 7922, 7930, 8391, 8700-8703, 10093, 13685, 14114, 14808, 14837, 15050, 15229, 15479-80

Joseph, Peter, 2753

Joshua, E.P., 15265

Kahn, Sam, 398, 3577, 3961, 4565, 8061, 9022, 9067, 9346-47, 9350-52, 9354-55, 9358-59, 9543, 14428

Kajee, Amin, 1280-81

Kathrada, Ahmed M., 112, 387-88, 391, 393, 398, 467, 481, 490, 510, 1062, 1068-70, 1125, 1209-10, 1280, 1284, 1332, 1408, 1411, 1460, 1493, 1494, 1851-53, 1860-61, 2227-28, 2345, 2356, 2489, 2540, 2573, 2583, 2663-64, 2705-6, 2709, 2890, 3090, 3598, 3610, 3633, 3675, 3677, 3888, 7462, 7468, 7664, 7669, 7945, 8328, 8339, 8372, 8389, 8438, 8442, 8561, 8587-89, 8703, 8768, 9229-30, 9305, 11052, 11300, 11832, 13538-40, 13689, 13776, 13788, 13891, 14022, 14062, 14114, 14790, 15049, 15066, 15076, 15088-89, 15115, 15128, 15282, 15561, 15577, 15586, 16141, 16151, 16527, 16569, 16806, 16809, 16879, 16930, 17075-76, 17126, 17214, 17239, 17240

Kazan, M., 1582

Keetse, P., 359-60

Keitsing, Fish, 504, 4127, 4299, 8950, 8962, 8997, 9182, 9186, 9295, 9301, 9319

Kepe, Lungile, 339, 3835, 3984, 3998, 9551, 9558, 9626, 9652, 9681, 9711, 9713, 9739, 9748, 9759, 9816, 9914, 15702, 16215, 16259, 16276, 16277, 18040

Khunou, Daniel, 7636, 9188

Komane, Mrs. Dora, 13989

Kosula, Sampson, 17811

Kotane, Moses, 354, 404, 558, 598, 688, 799, 811(a), 839, 949, 961, 1078, 1091, 1094, 1237, 1334, 1407, 1666, 1855, 2500, 2596, 2896, 2952, 2987, 2999, 3063, 3090, 3092, 3106-7, 3114, 3155, 3159, 3160(i), 3165, 3239, 3325, 3484-85, 3591-92, 3631, 3634, 3688, 3701, 3828, 3888, 3935, 3962, 4044, 4057, 4064, 4074, 4099, 4263, 4279, 4369, 4387, 4395, 4405, 4507, 4529, 7607, 8228-29, 8776, 8792, 8875, 8948, 9033-34, 9334, 9344, 9346, 9355, 9446-47, 9570, 9625, 9824, 10973, 11078, 11294, 11460, 11825, 11912, 13266-67, 13735-36, 13741, 14076-77, 14445, 14770, 15036, 15068-69, 15111, 15772, 16095-96, 16450, 16882, 17289, 17487, 17780, 17782-83, 18155, 18212

Kramer, Winifred, 2486, 4436-37

Kumalo, Jerry, 2527, 2532, 2942, 7560, 8898, 9165, 9232-33, 9337, 9578, 9580-81, 9752, 9859, 9863, 11252, 15157

Kumalo, Joseph M., 2649, 2774, 3183, 7736, 8204-6, 8224, 8231, 8238, 8241, 8248, 8258, 8265, 8268-69, 8271, 8273-74, 8276, 8278, 8293-94, 8300, 8304, 8312, 8314, 9167, 17006, 17153, 17387, 17432-33, 17725

La Guma, Alex, 510, 1437, 2736-37, 3696, 4069, 4120, 4539-40, 4542-43, 4547-48, 4579-80, 8075-76, 8078, 8087-88, 8091, 15355, 15438, 15528-29, 15550

La Guma, Jimmy, 9002, 9004, 9036, 9041, 9082, 9343, 9379, 9446, 17763

Lavoirrepierre, Mrs., 7989

Lawrence, V., 411, 440, 452, 999, 1029, 2585, 3685, 3699, 3745, 3747, 4444, 4590, 7988, 7997, 8012-13, 8048

Lazenger, Michael, 14855

Leballo, Potlako, 315, 856, 859, 860, 959, 982, 8890, 8915-16, 8924, 10916, 10920

Lee-Warden, L.B., 407, 1528, 1568, 1745, 1782, 1977, 2930, 3328, 3580, 3936, 4238, 9011-12, 9022, 9066-67, 13977, 14428, 14429, 15996, 17763

Lekeba, Joseph, 9860

Lengisi, J.M., 206, 277, 295, 1567, 3828, 9557, 9982

Letele, Dr. Arthur E., 345, 354, 360, 942, 1375, 2637, 2772, 2774-75, 2885, 3157-58, 3160(g), 3160(j), 3165-66, 3208, 3212, 3685, 3694, 3696, 4007, 4038, 4139, 4238, 8012, 10977, 11447, 11813, 11910, 17500, 17503, 17753, 17768, 17771, 18259

Letlaka, T.T., 326

Levy, Leon, 470, 922, 923, 1299, 1308, 1633, 1797, 1855, 1868, 1891, 1924-25, 2000, 2145,

2148-49, 2214-15, 2227-28,
2298, 2301, 2315-17, 2345,
2347, 2349, 2356, 2360, 2362,
2364, 2370, 2372, 2399-2400,
2404, 2406-7, 2410, 2412, 2421,
2489, 2506, 2511, 2700, 2745-
46, 3057, 3231, 3249, 3337-39,
3394, 3396-97, 3409, 3646,
4023, 4060, 4097, 4143, 4145,
4307, 4569, 7585-87, 7808,
7815, 7843, 7869, 7907-11,
8070-71, 8085, 8339, 8357,
8380, 8385, 8389, 8698, 8706-
7, 9031, 9099, 9105, 9452,
9970, 13024, 13111, 13453,
14435, 15558, 16151, 16748-
49, 16805

Levy, Norman, 363, 1581, 1582,
1583, 4086, 8706, 14466, 14498

Limbada, Dr., 14044-45

Lipman, Alan, 1782, 1853, 1855,
1861, 1954-66, 2347, 2356,
3576, 8338, 9353

Lollan, Stanley, 106, 1152-53,
1314-15, 1582, 1865, 2071,
2072, 2380, 2383, 2419, 2439,
3697, 3788, 3798, 3851, 4007,
4540, 6376-77, 7568, 7573,
7578, 7858-59, 7889, 7933-34,
8452, 8927, 8934, 9101, 9114-
15, 9453, 9970, 11824, 13760,
14412-13, 16712, 16720, 17418

Lovell, Leo, 4319, 4591, 8090

Lutuli (Luthuli), Albert J., 81, 211,
225, 226, 227, 242, 243, 245,
264, 267, 274, 275, 276, 289,
295, 304, 338, 345, 354, 362,
366, 378, 425, 440, 445, 488,
580, 611, 678-79, 725, 763,
798, 799, 856, 865, 924, 942,
984, 985, 994, 1000, 1021,
1026, 1028, 1029, 1034, 1042,
1076-77, 1080, 1094, 1194,
1200, 1322, 1375, 1400, 1434,
1437, 1471, 1474, 1480, 1580,
1584, 1588, 1749, 1854, 1862,
1911, 1927, 1998, 2015, 2016,
2019, 2021, 2034, 2053, 2057,

2066, 2077, 2078, 2197-98, 2236,
2283, 2567, 2586, 2602, 2612-
13, 2616, 2637, 2650, 2655, 2778,
2868, 2885, 2896, 2904, 2942,
2948, 2973, 3001, 3009, 3130,
3133, 3159, 3209, 3423-24, 3454,
3595-96, 3633, 3643, 3663-64,
3696, 3702, 3705, 3708, 3709,
3714, 3716, 3735, 3739(D), 3748,
3754, 3758, 3768, 3774, 3775,
3786, 3788, 3789, 3790, 3792,
3801, 3809, 3818, 3830, 3843,
3895, 3961, 3976, 3988, 3995,
4006-7, 4047, 4081, 4089-91,
4101, 4138, 4139, 4163, 4169,
4173, 4174, 4199, 4206, 4213,
4221, 4226, 4234, 4249, 4254,
4266, 4277, 4279, 4280, 4282,
4284, 4316, 4319, 4360, 4360(b),
4388, 4434, 4465, 4470, 4542,
4585, 4612-13, 7416, 7460, 7467,
7746, 7748, 7842, 8027, 8039,
8049-51, 8055, 8150, 8362, 8405,
8406, 8425, 8442, 8674, 8684,
8696, 8730-31, 8735, 8737, 8763,
8769, 8771, 8788, 8800, 8817,
8821, 8827, 8838, 8859, 8875,
8911, 8913-14, 8937, 8956, 8997,
9107, 9147, 9150, 9157, 9168,
9323, 9580, 9617, 9626, 9639,
9647, 9653, 9658, 9660, 9666-67,
9722, 9769, 9793, 9709, 9815,
9820, 9822, 9829, 9852-53, 9859,
9916, 9920, 9950, 9956, 9982,
9986, 10855, 10857-58, 10859,
10860, 10865, 10899, 10900,
10931, 10942, 10951, 10952,
10953, 10957, 10977, 11056,
11098, 11194, 11195, 11196,
11197, 11238, 11330, 11341,
11397, 11400, 11401, 11404,
11490, 11498, 11501, 11511,
11565, 11585, 11822-23, 11908-
10, 11932, 11949, 11979, 11993,
13020, 13074, 13283-86, 13530,
14080, 14147, 14412, 14659,
14691, 14876-79, 15478-79,
15633, 15634, 15669-74, 15732,
15733, 15739, 15740, 15741,
15742, 15754, 15755, 15758,
15829, 16203, 16264, 16322-23,
16339, 16420, 16449, 16450,
16487, 16575, 16576, 16667,
16679, 16680, 16681, 16684,

Lutuli, Albert J. (continued)
16703-4, 16793-94, 16808,
16979-82, 17011-12, 17064,
17066, 17070, 17072-73, 17144-
45, 17147, 17407, 17455, 17469,
17474, 17500, 17502, 17554,
17557, 17614, 17721, 17724,
17729-30, 17740, 17746, 17792,
17809, 17901, 17912, 17916,
17993, 17998, 18047, 18110,
18162, 18163, 18188, 18205,
18259, 18277, 18289

Maadi, A., 2084

Mabida, M.M., 2146, 8023, 11892,
11928, 17729-30

Macheke, G., 344

MacLeod, Hetty, 2137

McPherson, Mrs. Jesse, 1090,
1093

Madiba, Alpheus, 2952

Madzunya, I., 8795, 8846, 8848,
8855, 8857, 8859-60, 8875,
8917, 8919, 8922, 9936, 9939,
9942, 9944, 9952, 9955, 10053,
10066, 10916, 10920, 17371-
73, 17443

Mafeking, Elizabeth, 4090

Mafora, Jacob, 17796, 18110

Mahlangu, Aaron, 2149, 2315-18,
2774-75, 3250, 3382-83, 3385,
3398, 3409, 3981(b), 7808,
8883, 8888, 8898, 8904-5, 9337,
9582, 9585, 9604, 15157

Mahopo, David, 9321, 16824

Make, Vusumuzi, 2500, 2942, 3833,
3835, 8211-12, 8223-24, 8228,
8231, 8233, 8237-38, 8241, 8244,
8255, 8259, 8261-62, 8264,
8266, 8276, 8295, 8309, 8313,
8317-18, 9225, 14268, 16985,
17153, 17382

Makgothi, Henry G., 310, 325, 326,
344, 359-60, 378-79, 1858, 1983,
1985, 2053, 2228, 2356, 2580-
86, 3414, 3432, 4138, 4145, 7818,
8381, 8513-16, 8529, 8762-63,
8939, 9094, 9240, 9316, 9337,
11060, 11064-65, 11853, 13152-
53, 13528-29, 13557, 13589,
13702, 13813, 13815, 13817,
14837, 15229, 16019, 16129,
16236, 16237, 16238, 16239,
16241, 16248, 16256, 16320-21,
16829, 16992, 17003, 17141,
17172, 17173, 17174, 17268,
17332, 18231, 18250

Makiwane, Tennyson X., 886, 889,
1308, 1361, 2629, 2631-32, 2640,
2646, 2774, 4120, 4325, 8869-70,
8875, 9160-61, 9221-22, 9233,
9303, 9937, 9945, 9960, 9964,
13779, 14837, 15229, 16810,
16829, 17796

Makwe, Joshua, 3176, 3181, 9095,
9097, 9107-9, 9132, 14729,
16796-97, 17158, 17212, 17213

Malele, Elmon, 3227, 3230-31, 8804,
9580, 9582, 9852

Malindi, Z., 9047-48

Mall, Advocate H.E., 365-66, 525,
2930, 8043, 8722

Malupi, Sampi, 7588, 7639-41, 8890,
8949-52, 8959-60, 8964, 8993,
8997, 9150, 9169-70, 9185, 9187,
9219-21, 9295, 9298, 9301, 9319,
9322, 9324, 9327, 9337, 9452-53,
9625, 13535, 17158

Manana, P.J.S., 3672-73, 4180-81,
4184, 4200, 4521-22, 8808, 8818,
9028, 9036, 9071, 11304

Mancoko, L., 9676, 9763, 9770,
9801

Mandela, Nelson, 295, 404, 477,
688, 945, 946, 962, 994, 1780,
1901, 1904, 2023, 2248, 2835,
2836, 2837, 2894, 2907, 2908,

2911, 2922, 2923, 2924, 2928, 2952, 2970, 3412, 3419, 3469, 3473, 3534, 3573, 3578, 3591-92, 3828, 4326, 4393, 8339-40, 8501, 8545-48, 8775, 8952, 8988, 9134, 9242, 9321, 9335, 9557, 9570, 9872-73, 9878, 10058, 10088, 10973, 11062, 11072, 11087, 11188, 11200, 11201, 11203, 11231, 11585, 11813, 11815, 11918, 11922, 13120, 13126, 13153, 13157-58, 13161, 13196, 13227-29, 13231, 13236, 13372, 13570, 13591, 13598, 13643, 13788-91, 13795, 14145-46, 14541, 15067, 15582, 16347, 16377, 16455, 16483, 16490, 16541, 16568, 16569, 16681-83, 16702, 16802, 16865, 16894, 17285, 17413-14, 17500, 17576, 17787, 17815, 18053, 18057, 18066, 18232, 18251

Maponya, S., 2219

Marks, J.B., 295, 558, 598, 688, 950, 961, 1091, 1620, 1855, 2907, 2952, 3016, 3137, 3828, 3961, 4522, 7857, 8501, 8768, 8776, 8788, 8792, 8956, 8988, 9157, 9182, 9604, 9713, 9716, 10089-91, 10969, 11078, 13522, 13957, 14840, 15068, 15213-14, 15772, 16095, 16377, 16882, 17162, 17289, 17429, 18212

Maseko, MacDonald, 1861, 2486, 2698

Masemola, B.S., 1374, 1376, 3125, 3138, 8798, 8860, 8875, 9337, 9640, 9939, 9950-51, 9957-58, 9960

Mashaba, Bertha, 471, 2538, 2777, 2826, 3165, 3167-69, 3232, 3254, 4086, 4336, 4339, 4344, 7530, 7824, 9052, 9099, 9106, 9241, 9316, 9328, 13989, 14241, 14498, 16830

Mashaba, C., 339

Mashaba, July, 7564, 7736

Mashibini, Philemon, 217-18, 3801, 9511-12, 9514, 9517, 9521, 9729, 10088, 18261, 18262

Mashile, Janet B., 834, 963, 965, 1009, 2885, 4329, 4337, 8946, 8959

Masike, P., 3346

Massina, Leslie, 204, 345, 354, 470, 689, 818, 921, 943, 1309, 1361, 1375, 1635, 2145, 2147, 2298, 2318, 2340, 2356, 2375, 2407, 2409, 2628, 2736, 2774, 2960, 3229, 3249, 3315, 3317, 3331, 3334-38, 3339-40, 3343-49, 3390, 3396, 3404, 3448, 3457, 3872, 3889-90, 3927, 3977, 4060, 4165, 4341, 4355, 7591-92, 7607, 7630, 7632, 7736, 7846, 7893, 7997, 8010, 8045, 8048, 8184, 8357, 8381, 8417-18, 8453-54, 8696, 8701-2, 8882, 9103, 9124-25, 9335, 9452-53, 9570, 9583, 9586, 9605, 9969, 10903, 10977, 11014, 11231, 11620, 11814, 13656-58, 13685, 13788, 13986, 14839, 15230, 15436, 15558, 16065, 16200, 17061, 17127, 17264, 17425, 17427

Mateman, Don, 3249

Mathole, Philemon, 205, 224, 929, 1052, 1301, 1368, 1376, 1865, 2597-98, 2602-3, 2612, 2640-41, 2874, 2884, 2885, 2942, 3098, 3123, 3226, 3788, 3789, 4031, 4301, 4304, 4305, 4307, 4393, 4414, 7445-46, 7706, 7769-70, 7772, 8015, 8031, 8193, 8452, 8499, 8500, 8518, 8888, 9333, 9336, 9452, 9849, 9859, 9969, 10951, 11100, 11231, 11253, 11814, 11822-24, 11828, 11831, 11910, 13589, 13661, 13788, 15558, 16152, 16200, 16808, 16837, 17061, 17141, 17398, 17405, 17425, 17787-88

Mati, W., 339, 3997-98, 9470, 9551, 9555, 9651, 9717, 9737, 9742, 9994

Matji, Robert M., 212, 218, 276, 2991, 3828, 4470, 8860, 9528, 10002, 15136, 16302, 17904-5, 17971

Matlou, Jonas, 1206-7, 1213-14, 1219-20, 1361, 1997, 1999, 2024, 2025, 2626, 2775, 3139-40, 7883, 8933, 8953, 8955-57, 8960, 8971, 8979, 8986-87, 9096, 9148, 9228, 9231, 9237, 9575-76, 11279, 13538, 16541, 16774, 16985-86, 16995, 16997, 16998, 16999a, 17158, 17171, 17215, 17218, 17242, 17243, 17244, 17247, 17248

Matlou, Violet, 3141

Matomela, Mrs. Florence, 213, 471, 2137, 3776, 3796, 3815, 3849, 4016, 4019-20, 4328, 9652, 9653, 9799

Matseke, G., 359-60, 17141, 17421

Matshabi, John, 16377, 17425

Matthews, Joseph G., 326, 404, 2015, 2016, 2053, 2952, 3252, 3506, 3618, 3638, 3716, 3854, 4294, 4309, 4411, 4481, 4577, 9531, 9611, 9615, 9641, 10918, 10919, 10922, 10999, 11064, 11065, 11069, 11288, 11289, 11307, 11309, 11851, 11910, 13153, 13255-56, 13258, 13260, 14790-91, 15453-54, 15695, 16096, 16356, 17754, 17769-70, 18040-41, 18175

Matthews, Professor Z.K., 212, 277, 345, 363, 366, 612, 688, 699, 820, 994, 1028, 1029, 1489, 1491, 1666, 2066, 2885, 3593, 3668, 3774, 3775, 3786, 3787, 3789, 3796, 3797, 3828, 3849, 4199, 4363, 4455-56, 4464, 4470-71, 4476-81, 4596, 4598, 4611, 9480, 9482, 9557, 9611, 9636, 9640, 9646-47, 9731, 9769, 9807-8, 10869, 10870, 10977, 11103, 11681, 11682, 11813, 13014, 13020, 13022-23, 13108-9, 13111, 13113-25, 13164, 13208, 13260, 13262, 13291, 13372, 13378-79, 13591-13602, 13904-5, 14782-83, 15588, 15757, 15777, 16982, 17125, 17501, 17503, 17576, 17612, 18199, 18309

Mavuso, John S.A., 404, 2631, 2640, 2775, 2908, 3116-17, 3206, 3220-23, 8787, 8792, 8796, 8842, 17160, 17370, 17438-39

Mayekiso, C., 361, 470, 790, 819, 932, 940, 943, 944, 983, 1034, 1375, 2315-17, 2774, 3776, 3797, 3798, 3802, 3807, 3810, 3812, 3815, 3833, 3835, 3846, 3850, 3860, 3872-73, 4013, 4165, 9470, 9477, 9538, 9565, 9617, 9619, 9623, 9641, 9651-52, 9656, 9664, 9696-97, 9710, 9721-23, 9727, 9729, 9734, 9751, 9755, 9768-70, 9785, 9790, 9910, 9924, 10006, 10029, 11231, 11910, 11928, 15623, 15661, 15702, 15707, 15719, 15737(c), 15742, 16157, 16223, 16226, 16227, 16266, 16272, 16333-35, 16355, 18033, 18085, 18100

Mayekiso, George, 212, 15632-33

Mayet, S.M., 2562, 3675

Mbeki, Govan, 3222, 3872-74, 4085, 4087, 4098

Mbelekana, Z., 9912, 9924

Mda, A.P., 1666, 4204, 10060, 10062, 17576-77, 17579, 18309

Meer, A.I., 526

Meer, Ismail, 403, 423, 452, 2562, 77, 8027, 17580

Meer, Mrs. Ismail (Fatima), 423

Mei, Pious G., 2315-17, 8823

Mekgoe, D., 3346

Meti, Abel, 9946, 9949, 9952, 9955

Mfaxa, Elliot, 3979, 9482, 9559, 9729, 9730, 9740, 9918-19, 10954, 15639

Mgungunyeka, David, 4492, 4496, 4498, 4581, 8078, 8080, 8092, 9050

Mhlaba, Raymond, 3828, 9619, 9718-19, 9751

Mini, V., 339, 3812, 3833, 3982-84, 3996-97, 4273, 9484, 9486-87, 9551, 9663, 9678, 9688, 9698-99, 9701, 9725-26, 9743, 9749, 9756, 9819, 15685, 15702, 15707, 16215, 16234, 16259, 16276, 16289, 16340, 16355, 18041-42, 18099-18101, 18262

Mistry, D.U., 529, 605, 995, 1434, 2077

Mji, Dr. D., 244, 326, 404, 2939, 3075, 3076, 3136, 3828, 3860, 4450, 4464, 9470, 11813-15, 11972-73, 11975, 13071, 13091, 13128, 13143, 13145, 15661-66, 15668, 15735, 15756, 16842-43, 18219, 18247

Mkalipi, S.P., 3807, 3808, 3809, 4013, 9460, 9462, 9467-69, 9537-38, 9545, 9548, 9565, 9567, 9623, 9701-2, 9902-4, 9906, 9914, 9919, 9921-22, 10030, 11231, 15630, 15659, 15672, 15679, 16158, 16306, 16357, 16360, 16712-14, 16716, 18262

Mkize, Mrs. Bertha, 1939, 8818

Mkwanazi, Lillian, 9965, 10058

Mkwayi, Wilton, 339, 3815, 3833, 3851, 3865-66, 3870, 3873, 3984, 4013, 4273, 4274, 9499, 9505-6, 9541, 9561-62, 9567, 9615, 9619, 9641-42, 9651, 9659, 9664, 9668, 9671, 9694, 9699, 9719, 9727, 9729, 9735, 9738-39, 9750, 9760, 9764, 9766, 9770-71, 9790, 9799, 9818, 9837, 9913, 9919, 10033, 11231, 11910, 12070, 12084, 13053, 13780-81, 15623, 15684, 15707, 15720, 15737(c), 15743, 15885, 16158, 16224, 16228, 16230, 16267, 16272, 16328, 16335-38, 16355, 18035, 18262

Mmusi, Theophilus, 8953, 8961, 8964, 9183-84, 9190, 9302

Mngoma, V., 3197, 4332, 4333, 4334, 7551, 7580, 8379, 8412, 9966, 15423

Modiba, Frank, 2593, 2620, 8948, 8951-52, 9135, 9146, 9149, 9874, 11878, 17157, 17477

Modise, Johannes, 4413, 7489, 7822, 7824-26, 8564, 8943, 8946, 8958, 9163, 9238, 9241, 9300, 9315, 9325, 16541, 16991, 17207, 17216

Moiloa, David, 9135, 9238, 10082, 10087

Mokgofe, Piet, 8957, 8959, 9178, 9225-26, 9301, 9307-8, 9312, 9322, 9725

Molaoa, Patrick, 310, 316, 1983, 2650-52, 2654, 7518, 7521, 7819, 7968, 8890, 8927, 8930-31, 8942, 8946, 8952, 8958, 8961, 8968, 8981, 9096, 9099, 9228, 9239, 9241, 9317, 11231, 16152, 16828, 16991, 17280

Molapo, Nathan, 1515, 4135

Molema, Dr. S.M., 525, 527, 688, 1853, 3068, 3197, 3828

Moletsane, Emily, 7588

Molewa, B., 2640, 7429, 8801, 8842, 8873, 8877, 8923, 9937, 9940-41, 17418

Molife, Joseph, 2655, 2658-59, 2709-10, 2932, 2933, 2936, 2939, 2942, 2950, 2951, 3074, 3076, 4043, 8212-13, 8223, 8225-28, 8237-38, 8241, 8243, 8249, 8251, 8256, 8258, 8261, 8264-65, 8271, 8294, 8298, 8304-5, 8312-13, 8317, 8490, 8771-73, 8775, 8779, 8792-93, 8805-6, 8871, 8888-89, 9163, 9793, 10009, 11165, 11231, 11252, 11263, 14729, 14744, 14821, 15155, 15558, 16152, 16802, 16828, 17015, 17153

Moloela, Isron, 9222

Molotsi, Peter, 315

Monanyane, Leslie, 4428-29, 4431-33

Mongul, S.B., 526, 1154

Moola, Ebrahim, 1061, 1070, 1210, 1217-20, 3183, 7407, 8700-8701, 15117-18

Moolla, Moosa (Mosie), 111, 387-88, 391, 467, 513, 790, 944, 1062, 1064, 1066, 1143, 1209-10, 1221-22, 1227-28, 1300, 1316, 1318, 1319, 1320, 1328, 1330, 1361, 1449, 1492, 1793, 1855, 1926, 2343, 2347, 2445, 2478, 2649, 2657, 2663, 2668, 2676, 2681, 2688, 2711, 2726, 2739, 2752, 2755-59, 2773, 2847, 3159, 3323, 3598, 3660, 3665, 3671, 3680, 3777, 3793, 3977, 3985, 4027, 4056, 4165, 4430, 4537, 7512-14, 7637, 7967-68, 8323-24, 8328, 8362, 8372, 8381, 8422-23, 8700, 9239, 14412-13, 14835, 14837, 15118, 15230, 15561, 16153, 16928, 17276, 17277, 17278, 17279

Moonsamy, Keswel, 4189, 4240, 4243, 8045

Moosa, Hassen M., 921, 943, 1064, 1068, 1143, 1318, 1323, 1324, 1325, 1326, 1327, 1333, 1349, 1581, 1856, 2059, 2078, 2227-28, 2375, 2628, 2736, 4027, 4097, 4234, 7429, 7487, 7851, 7860, 7946, 8328, 8452, 9010, 9238, 15082, 15088, 15229, 16540, 17142

Moosa, Mrs. M., 3255

Moosagee, M., 1300, 1330

Moretsele, Elias P., 204, 276, 310, 359, 361, 822, 823, 931, 942, 943, 1034, 1051, 1334, 1337, 1375, 1675, 1855, 1856, 1983, 2059, 2228, 2345-47, 2610, 2613, 2620, 2626-27, 2701-2, 2885, 2886, 2907, 3525, 3581, 3786, 3788, 4027, 4134, 4138, 4144, 4299, 7434-36, 7849-50, 7900, 7993, 8131, 8182-85, 8243, 8358, 8363, 8429, 8434, 8452, 8480-81, 8517-20, 8522, 8535, 8701, 8806, 8887, 8919, 9169, 9332, 9452, 9857, 9874, 9970-71, 10087, 10091, 10100, 10902, 10903, 10951, 10977, 11093, 11231, 11234, 11252, 11300, 11814, 11818, 11822-23, 11825, 11829-30, 11911-12, 13382-83, 13656, 13658, 13788, 14412, 14836, 15560, 16065, 16153, 16199, 16575, 16576, 16808, 16928, 16982, 17005, 17066, 17127, 17140, 17141-42, 17398, 17405, 17425, 17431, 17815, 17933

Moretsele, Mrs. Elias P., 344, 345

Moroka, Dr. James S., 959, 980, 1029, 1396, 1397, 2589, 3075, 8800, 8854-55, 9617, 9872, 10089, 11636, 15067, 15777, 15818, 16015, 17899, 18026, 18261

Morolong, Joseph, 4505, 4548, 4565, 8915, 9051-52, 9085

Morris, Fred, 204, 1635, 2066, 2942, 4305, 8357, 8868, 17141, 17773

Morrison, Lionel, 1361, 2375, 4543, 4547-48, 8701-2, 8902, 9039, 9582, 9599-9600, 9602, 15368, 15531-32

Motala, Dr. Mohamed M., 525, 1071, 1318, 1183, 1419, 1919, 2692, 3658, 3665, 3682, 3695, 3699, 3750, 4166, 4176-79, 4216, 4236, 4237, 4238, 4239, 4242, 8023, 8040, 8725, 8733, 8739, 8815, 11879, 11893

Motlana, Dr. Harrison, 3075, 3076, 16802, 16865, 17557

Motlhakwana, Mrs. Martha, 3160(j), 4326, 4327, 4339, 4344

Motloheloa, J.S.P., 2068

Motsele, Michael, 8214, 8223, 8231, 8238, 8266, 8305, 8345, 8764, 8767, 8775, 8790-91, 8795, 8797, 8803, 8848, 8911, 8915, 9942-44, 9959, 10054, 10058, 10066, 17368-73, 17434-35, 17438-43, 17452

Motshabi, D., 1205, 4331, 4334

Motshabi, J., 276, 2907, 2908, 3828, 4393, 8321, 17141, 17406

Motshabi, Obed, 344, 359-60, 1218-20, 1361, 3093, 3226, 4321, 4394, 7736, 7881, 9573-74, 9759, 9847, 9851, 9854, 9862, 9868, 9870, 11829, 16929, 17159, 17373, 17406, 17421

Moumakoe, Esther, 9578, 9752, 10093

Mpanza, J.S., 2623

Mphahlele, Ezekiel, 943, 1309, 3250

Mphosho, Gladys, 9964-65

Mqota, T.D., 3995, 3999, 9550, 15739, 16368, 18042-43

Msimang, Selby, 1666, 4204, 7406-7

Mtini, John, 4503, 4505, 4506, 8065-66, 8082, 9024, 9027, 9029, 9031, 9068-69, 9074, 9082, 9113

Mtwa, H., 226, 9626

Mtwana, Ida, 1620, 1935, 1939, 1941, 2248, 4333, 4334, 8888, 8992, 9311, 9337, 9460, 13989, 14839, 15213, 15608, 17127, 17406

Mutton, A.J., 2930, 3786

Naicker, Dr. G.M., 235, 403-4, 411, 423, 437, 440, 452, 544, 689, 950, 994, 1061-62, 1070, 1209, 1284-85, 1322, 1323, 1328, 1434, 1437, 1454, 1470, 1476, 1479, 1500, 1504, 1597-98, 1602, 1607, 1698, 1701, 1854, 1862, 1904, 1928-30, 2042, 2043, 2050, 2075, 2077, 2078, 2079, 2493, 2506, 2561, 2562, 2567, 2577, 2586, 2736, 3597, 3609, 3635, 3657, 3663, 3675-77, 3681, 3687, 3690, 3695, 3696, 3697, 3699, 3701, 3726, 3727, 3729, 3733, 3734, 3743, 3745, 3746, 3747, 3755, 3758, 3759, 3761, 3762, 3763, 3791, 3840, 3953, 4192-93, 4216, 4219, 4220, 4225, 4236, 4238, 4243, 4244, 4246, 4254, 4279, 4284, 4319, 4591, 7667, 7842-43, 7988, 7993, 7998, 8005, 8013, 8027, 8039-40, 8051-52, 8054, 8726, 8733, 9969, 10899, 10943, 10951, 11485, 11651, 11830, 13274, 14981-82, 15023, 15067, 15073, 15082, 15111, 15117, 15228, 15300, 16470, 17123, 17474, 17501, 17503-4, 17555, 17580, 17692, 17709-10, 17719

Naicker, M.P., 403, 423, 452, 525, 1927, 2561, 3620, 3657, 3661, 3668-69, 3672-73, 3676-77, 3711, 3713, 3736, 3737, 3791, 4139, 4183, 4194, 4220, 4238, 4246, 4362, 7607, 7990, 8015, 8031, 10943, 13274, 13787, 15049, 15082

Naicker, Narainsamy T., 111, 112, 364, 420, 513, 515, 942, 1307, 1375, 1755, 2494, 3654, 3677, 3680, 3682, 3690, 3694, 3695, 3699, 3734, 4008, 4167, 4214, 4215, 4218, 4219, 4234, 4235, 4236, 4237, 4238, 4239, 4240, 4241, 4242, 4244, 4245, 4246, 7997, 8006-7, 8012-13, 8023, 8031, 8708, 8721, 8725-26, 8732, 8738, 8747, 10943, 10955, 11295, 11331, 15083

Naidoo, R.D., 528

Naidoo, S.R., 452, 8231

Naidoo, T.N., 2346, 2489, 15073, 15213, 16569, 16570

Nair, Billy, 488, 1284, 1928, 2315, 2561, 2592, 3658, 3673, 3677-78, 3682, 3695, 3697, 3698, 3699, 4185-86, 4189, 4194, 4237, 4238, 4245, 4246, 4570, 8011, 8015, 14044, 15050, 15082

Nathie, Suliman, 7159, 8211, 8213, 8233, 8237-38, 8268-69, 8273-74, 8297, 8303-4

Ndimba, B., 3807, 3883, 9489, 9500, 9537, 9544-46, 9548, 9567, 9634, 9699, 9762, 9912, 9916, 10012-13, 10017, 10019-22, 10028-29, 11231, 11240, 13651, 13654-55, 13831, 14080, 14155, 14804, 15616-19, 15623, 15632, 15656, 15696, 15697, 15699, 15702, 15706, 15711, 15713, 15718, 15727, 15728, 15744, 15749, 15750, 15750(a), 15940, 16159, 16251, 17068-69, 17474, 17712, 18035, 18238

Nene, Phineas, 499, 1374, 2630, 3094, 8773, 8779, 8789, 8791, 8795-96, 8802, 8813, 8839, 8846, 8854, 8857-60, 8865, 9938, 9960, 9964, 10061, 11231, 13522, 14084, 16154, 17370, 17438-39

Ngakane, Lionel, 7962, 16129

Ngotyana, Greenwood, 213, 1334, 2680, 2882, 3160(i), 3165, 3776, 3790, 3796, 3798, 3801, 3887, 4484, 4487, 4491, 4565, 4581, 4601, 9016, 9018, 9022, 10047

Ngoyi, Mrs. Lillian, 344, 471, 510, 789, 921, 1310, 1369, 1752, 1796, 1851-53, 1861, 1946, 2132, 2134, 2384, 2445, 2459, 2506, 2509, 2517, 2518, 2611, 2627, 2637, 2736, 2777, 2826, 2867, 2874, 3165, 3172, 3229, 3232, 3253, 3255, 4052, 4300, 4333, 4334, 4339, 4344, 4347, 4355, 4367, 4380-83, 4385, 4387, 4395, 4451, 7420, 7595, 7653, 7851, 7887, 8234, 8380, 8452, 8535, 8904, 9098, 9166, 9180, 9452, 9574, 9582, 9586, 9968, 9970, 11017, 11018, 11231, 11911, 13022, 13329, 13685, 13764, 13788, 13817, 13989, 14066, 14068, 14107, 14114, 14189, 14238, 14351-52, 14726, 14808-9, 14820-24, 14828, 14832-33, 14836, 15066, 15431, 15437, 15528, 15719, 16154, 17141, 17260, 17261, 17264, 17387, 17406, 17425, 17796, 17815

Ngubane, Jordan, 3474, 4047, 4200, 4203-5, 11394, 17566, 17579

Ngwane, Gilbert, 9851, 9860-63

Ngwendu, Robert, 3184, 3216, 8934

Ngwendu, William A., 344, 4125-26, 8439, 8518, 8934, 9148, 9317, 10092, 16774, 16818, 16824, 16991, 16995, 16997, 17141, 17188, 17198

Ngwentshe, 206, 3828, 3883, 4521-22, 7849, 9515, 9557, 9806, 9982

INDEXES

Ngwenya, Thomas, 1264, 2690, 2909, 2942, 3849, 7406-7, 9010-11, 9014, 9059, 17501, 17503, 17762, 18262

Ngwevela, Johnson, 558, 598, 990, 3828, 3961, 13957, 17761, 17780, 17782

Nhlabati, L.K., 1666

Nhlandhlo, Phineas, 15588

Nhlapo, Walter, 928

Njongwe, Dr. James, 212, 276, 503, 688, 2991, 3618, 3774, 3775, 3776, 3803, 3810, 3816, 3828, 3849, 3878, 4221, 8674, 8860, 9617-19, 9624-25, 9633, 9637, 9640, 9642, 9718, 9751, 9810, 10002, 15140, 15639, 15756, 15757, 16302, 17513, 17763, 17906, 17912, 17916, 18261, 18262, 18275, 18276, 18287

Nkadimeng, John N., 144-45, 344, 359-60, 437, 467, 470, 927, 945, 1205, 1785, 1998, 2084, 2315, 2318-19, 2361, 2400, 2486, 2489, 2491, 2530, 2620, 2699, 3240, 3396, 3402-3, 4302, 4438, 7779, 7807, 7871, 8150, 8154, 8184, 8186, 8205, 8294, 8345, 8350, 8454, 8887, 10903, 11231, 11238, 11910, 11928, 13658, 13788, 14836, 15156, 15229, 16154, 16200, 17061, 17127, 17141, 17398, 17776

Nkampeni, J., 9538, 9546, 9565, 9653, 9655, 9703, 9766, 9787-88, 9815, 9837, 9840, 9917, 9923, 9925-26, 11231, 15623, 16159, 16354, 18035, 18262

Nkatlo, Joseph, 9343, 9348, 9446

Nkosi, Lawrence, 379, 3116, 3118, 3122-23, 3204, 4304, 4320, 7560, 7736, 7743, 7748, 7779, 7782, 7808, 8884, 9335-36, 9572-74, 9582, 9859, 9861, 9863

Nobadula, F.P., 9097

Nogaya, A.B., 4011-13, 9537, 9540, 9545, 9548-49, 9551, 9559, 9907-8, 9925-26, 10043, 15615, 15630, 18043

Nokwe, P.P. Duma, 138, 306, 307, 308, 316, 326, 404, 510, 644, 829, 833, 840, 866, 1940-41, 1946, 2184, 2375, 2397, 2599, 2625, 2632, 2760, 2771, 2779, 2796, 2807, 2838, 2840, 2848, 2850, 2851, 2852, 2853, 2854, 2855, 2856, 2857, 2882, 2883, 3090-91, 3093, 3160(g), 3160(i), 3164, 3256, 3412, 3570, 3595, 3610-11, 3638, 3783, 3812, 3833, 3834, 3835, 3842, 4262, 4268, 4329, 4336, 4341, 4343, 4435-36, 7657, 7922, 8143, 8150, 8321, 8494, 8500, 8511, 8531-32, 8701, 8770, 8787, 9804, 9856, 9858, 10093, 10095, 11012, 11052, 11063, 11065, 11231, 11237, 11949, 13011, 13111, 13114, 13116-17, 13121-24, 13145, 13329, 13415, 13483, 13658, 13685, 13689, 13777, 13903, 13905, 14114, 14129, 14209-10, 14808, 14813-14, 15703, 16019, 16129, 16155, 16181, 16199, 16540, 16580, 16804, 16828, 16897, 17061-64, 17119, 17761, 17792, 17929

Nthithe, Peter P., 310, 1983, 3244-45, 8437, 8939-40, 8942, 8947, 8957, 8978, 8991, 9096, 9159, 9226, 9240, 9337, 9461, 9863, 9870, 16541, 16829, 16986, 16989, 16991-92, 16996, 17171, 17207, 17216, 17230, 17231, 17233, 17776

Ntsangani, Milner, 339, 3833, 3979, 3984, 9540, 9543, 9616, 9624, 9635, 9641, 9653, 9655, 9658-70, 9672, 9675-76, 9680, 9687-88, 9701, 9705, 9707, 9721, 9793, 9797-98, 9800, 9840, 9924, 11231, 15624, 15656, 15715, 15737(c), 15744, 15750(a), 15752, 16159, 16204, 16712-13, 16715, 18036, 18262

Nyembe, Dorothy, 1999, 4170, 8813

Nyembe, G. Dumisa, 225, 8809-10, 8814, 17469, 17488, 17533

Nzo, Alfred, 2631, 2640, 2775

Omar, Dr., 525

Padayachee, Dr., 388, 412, 1061-63, 1070, 1454, 2561, 3660, 3682, 3687, 3696, 3699, 3744, 3746, 4220, 4234, 4235, 4236, 4237, 4238, 4239, 4240, 4242, 4244, 8013, 15082, 15117

Palmer, Miss Josie, 1942, 2137, 2384, 2517

Patel, Ahmed E., 111, 204, 363-65, 513, 942, 1116, 1142-43, 1212-13, 1217, 1283, 1304, 1361, 1375, 1591, 1635, 1865, 2059, 2595-96, 2604, 2886, 2942, 3159, 3675, 3680, 3696, 3697, 4007, 4139, 4234, 4430, 7934, 7990, 8005, 8039-40, 8338, 8357-58, 8555, 9134, 9873, 10951, 11831, 15088, 15173, 16540, 16808, 17159, 17512

Paton, Alan, 8052, 17150

Peake, George, 942, 1375, 3976, 4008, 4139, 4510, 4541, 4543, 4545, 4547, 4549, 9027, 9037, 9043, 9046, 9081, 15315-16, 15318, 15478, 15531

Petersen, A., 9118

Phillips, James, 3250, 9862, 15355

Pillay, V.S.M., 363, 451, 1026, 2219, 2315-16, 2318, 3673, 3676-77, 3681-82, 3695, 3697, 3698, 3699, 4235, 4236, 4237, 4238, 4239, 4242, 4243, 4246, 4285, 4286, 4293, 7997, 8003, 8010-11, 8709, 8714-15, 14839, 15082

Pitje, G.M., 15776

Press, Dr. Ronald E., 363, 942, 1218-19, 1375, 1581, 1582, 2083, 2182, 2316, 2478, 2506, 2511, 2701, 2725, 2736, 2773, 3033, 3117, 4038, 4404, 4408, 4411-12, 4453, 6375-76, 7509-10, 7512, 7573, 7619-20, 7864, 7967, 8219, 8278, 8358, 8391, 8452, 8491, 8698, 8928, 8953-54, 8986, 9104, 9126, 9239, 9970, 13760, 14436, 14438, 14615-16, 14622, 14727, 14729, 14837, 17159, 17273, 17275, 17445

Price, Professor T.W., 518, 1393, 3469-73, 11203, 11204, 13230-36, 13643, 13788, 13790-92, 13795, 13841, 14145-47, 14150-51, 16490, 16681-83, 16702

Putini, Y., 2611, 7968, 9099, 10969, 17140

Radebe, Gaur, 15776

Rahim, S.M., 1283

Ralphs, Sheila, 8365

Rantha, Mrs. Mary, 471, 1255-56, 2132, 2360-61, 2777, 3253, 4302, 4304, 4322, 4325, 4327, 4328, 4339, 4342, 4343, 4344, 7562, 7736, 7750, 7889, 8249-50, 8454, 8938-39, 10932, 16992

Reddy, S.V., 423, 527

Reeves, Bishop Ambrose, 11488, 17830

Resha, Robert, 143-44, 147, 223, 225, 310, 326, 344, 345, 359-62, 364, 378, 467, 482, 490, 680, 719, 763, 764, 765, 769, 770, 786, 792, 817, 943, 946, 1217, 1369, 1511, 1706, 1982, 2015, 2016, 2053, 2069, 2120, 2486, 2489, 2583, 2650, 2656, 2701, 2705-6, 2708, 2774-75, 2816, 2885, 2911, 2971, 3099, 3120, 3159, 3160(j), 3165, 3179-8

INDEXES

3232, 3253, 3255, 3258-59,
3416-17, 3638, 3680, 3779,
3786, 3787, 3788, 3789, 3824,
3910, 3920, 3924, 3980(3981a),
4086, 4142, 4146, 4299, 4302,
4332, 4336, 4343, 4541, 7478,
7492, 7501, 7503, 7525, 7582,
7584, 7597, 7824-25, 7830,
7859, 7860, 7934, 7937, 7948,
7992, 8005-6, 8023, 8026,
8029, 8149, 8184, 8186, 8218,
8232, 8321, 8337, 8339-40,
8345, 8362, 8364, 8366, 8377,
8379-80, 8399, 8406, 8408,
8412, 8424, 8426, 8442, 8452,
8483, 8509-10, 8559, 8560,
8566, 8674, 8677-78, 8734,
8741, 8762, 8779-80, 8885,
8927, 8931, 8935, 8937, 8942,
8947, 8955, 8967, 8973, 8978,
8988, 9048, 9051, 9087-88,
9098, 9135, 9152, 9157, 9165,
9167, 9181, 9226, 9238-39,
9241, 9298, 9316, 9473-74,
9516, 9519, 9576, 9586, 9641-
42, 9644, 9646, 9811, 9813,
9874, 9919, 9949-50, 9953,
10006, 10012, 10036, 10055-56,
10082, 10092, 10095-97, 10099,
10903, 10951, 10953, 10954,
10957, 10977, 10978, 11052,
11053, 11070, 11071, 11072,
11080, 11231, 11234, 11236,
11238, 11239, 11252, 11253,
11255, 11268, 11276, 11328,
11404, 11813-14, 11822-24,
11827, 11828, 11832, 11851,
13162, 13510, 13524, 13533-
34, 13546, 13551, 13557, 13559,
13589, 13655-56, 13659-60,
13662-63, 13689, 13770, 13778,
13780, 13788, 13816-17, 13945,
14034, 14052, 14062, 14178,
14415, 14498, 14656-57, 14682,
14803, 14805, 14837, 14848,
14873-74, 15300, 15365, 15414,
15424, 15431-33, 15496, 15522,
15531, 15557-58, 15560, 15563,
15643, 15724, 15737(g), 15753,
15785, 15788, 16004, 16027,
16065, 16149, 16155, 16256,
16303, 16320, 16808, 16868,
16982, 17198, 17207, 17208,
17226, 17228, 17229-34, 17236,
17237, 17259, 17266, 17269,
17270, 17271, 17398, 17405,
17422, 17427, 17430-31, 17451,
17730, 17745, 17776, 17796,
17933, 18043, 18046, 18054,
18154

Rietstein, Miss Amy, 2144

Routh, Guy, 7462, 8230, 8232,
    8337, 8424, 14848, 16032, 16034

Roux, Edward, 1782, 14857, 17541

Sachs, E.S. (Solly), 15349

Sacks, Betty, 18196

Sader, Dr. A., 942, 1328, 1375,
    2561, 2592, 3657, 3682, 4008,
    4165, 4237, 4242, 10942, 15082

Saleh, Salim, 1858, 2486

Saloojee, I.M., 6473, 16569, 16570

Scott, Michael, 952, 2952, 3686,
    3691, 8039, 9149, 17349-50

Seedat, Dawood A., 1636, 1642,
    1894, 1919-20, 2084, 2219,
    2246, 2356, 2561, 2592, 3090,
    3657, 3676, 3678, 3682, 3695,
    3698, 3699, 3738, 3739, 3739(A),
    4235, 4236, 4237, 4242, 4244,
    4246, 4247, 4276, 4319, 8008,
    8014-15, 8712-14, 8716, 8746-
    47, 8756, 8758, 11007, 11293,
    14838, 15049, 15082, 15229,
    17583

Seedat, Fatima, 1904, 8821, 8827,
    14815

Segal, Ronald, 14858

Seichoareng, Abraham, 2284, 4445,
    17753, 17768

Seitshiro, Bennett, 8961, 8963,
    9171, 9185, 9221, 9304, 9320,
    9324, 9326, 13535, 14127

Sejake, Nimrod, 481, 1642, 2084, 2317, 2477, 3115, 3118, 3212, 3225-26, 3403, 4022, 6375, 7573-74, 7578, 7808, 8378-79, 8382, 8413, 8427, 8429, 11231, 11277, 13760, 14024, 15325-27, 15330, 15340, 15364-65, 15414-17, 15563, 16567, 16720, 17160, 17248

Selby, Arnold, 1780

Selepe, Peter, 504, 3316-17, 8804-5, 8840, 8864, 8867, 8879, 8881, 9569, 9573, 9586, 9605, 11231, 14112, 16157

Seperepere, Marupeng, 1851, 1861, 15020

September, Reginald, 4535-40, 4542-43, 4547-49, 8071, 8077, 8085, 8088, 9002, 9004, 9343, 15266

Sesedi, 17753, 17768, 17771

Shall, Sydney, 1206, 1219-21, 2701, 2705, 2707, 2939, 3074, 3389, 4368, 8391, 8419-21, 8762, 8766, 11832, 13775, 14436, 15376, 16528, 16806, 16929-30, 17015, 17020

Shanley, Errol, 8005, 8045, 8055, 8733

Shope, Marks W., 2315-19, 3338-39, 3343-49, 3409, 4301, 4304, 4305, 7406-7, 7556, 7727, 7736, 7950, 8194, 8200, 8518, 9847, 9867, 17061

Sibande, Cleopas, 2148-49, 2315-17, 3248, 4060, 8070, 8083, 9094-95, 9097, 9099, 9119, 11911

Sibande, Gert, 205, 277, 344, 404, 2658, 2698-99, 2907, 4522, 7772, 7779, 7859, 7868, 7900, 8248, 8252, 8259, 8278, 8302-3, 8318, 8452, 8790, 8792, 9165, 9333, 9453, 9970, 11250,
13621, 13788, 13944, 14837, 15213, 15438, 15558, 16065, 16157, 16571, 17006

Sibea, Rev. J.M., 226

Sibeko, Archibald, 4581, 9579

Silinga, Mrs. Annie, 1334, 9027, 9031

Simons, H.J., 919, 1169, 1264, 2124, 2461, 2690, 2909, 2942, 3672, 3702, 4360(d), 4507, 4570, 14428, 14450, 14451, 15130, 17482-83, 15847, 15849, 16094, 16097

Singh, Debi, 403, 423, 451-52, 522, 525, 526, 2077, 2078, 2248, 3620, 3669, 3675-76, 8027, 15049, 15073, 15173, 15201-6, 17691

Singh, J.N., 423, 440, 3676-77, 11651

Sisulu, Walter, 150, 202, 208, 274, 276, 290, 404, 444, 510, 513, 599, 602, 604, 605, 673, 829, 854, 864, 928, 929, 950, 994, 1858, 1860, 1895, 1939, 1941, 2065, 2226-27, 2231, 2260, 2337, 2397, 2400, 2561, 2562, 2567, 2568, 2586, 2625, 2751, 2816, 2826, 2876, 2882, 2883, 2884, 2953, 2955, 2960, 2965, 2985, 2991, 3090-91, 3113, 3156, 3438, 3475, 3476, 3536, 3555, 3571, 3577, 3581-82, 3586, 3589, 3596, 3599-3600, 3606, 3608, 3610, 3613-15, 3618, 3637, 3649, 3675, 3701, 3726, 3774, 3775, 3789, 3790, 3795, 3798, 3801, 3826, 3867-68, 3888, 3986, 4263, 4268, 4270, 4446, 4458, 4480, 4491, 7923, 8340-41, 8360, 8399, 8442, 8562, 8785, 8787, 8789, 8792, 8875, 8956, 8988, 9168, 9511-13, 9517, 9621, 9623, 9625, 9637-38, 9791, 9810, 9820, 9823-24, 9834-35, 9838, 10092-93, 10095-97, 10977, 10978, 11062, 11103, 11104, 11171, 11231, 11813

11814, 11818, 11824, 11827,
11853, 13140, 13154, 13247,
13329, 13420, 13522, 13530,
13685, 13788, 13905, 14114,
14412, 14808, 14837, 15018,
15111, 15300, 15301, 15414,
15703, 15707-8, 15709, 15710,
15780, 15785, 15786, 15851,
16157, 16199, 16320, 16414,
16580, 16793, 16804, 16897,
16971-72, 17011-12, 17062,
17500, 17503, 17545, 17676,
17763, 17899, 18046-47, 18075,
18222, 18232, 18248, 18278,
18289, 18308

Sita, Nana, 437, 688, 994, 1434,
1853, 2984, 3068, 8233

Skomolo, J.J., 441, 17639

Slachter, Mrs. Rose, 14866

Slovo, Joseph, 162, 404, 1528,
1568, 1782, 2085, 2086, 2657,
2674, 2848, 3117, 3231, 3239,
3788, 7434, 7446-47, 7918,
7993, 8391, 8419-20, 9643,
10016, 10950, 11824, 11830,
14412, 14437, 14492, 14790,
17070, 17512, 17691

Slovo, Ruth First, 404, 510, 516,
518, 743, 829, 830, 919, 1415,
1418, 1430, 1528, 1568, 1620,
1652, 1782, 1855, 1858, 1861,
1896-97, 1958, 2084, 2085,
2125, 2224-25, 2227-28, 2267,
2293, 2345, 2356, 2397, 2402,
2486, 2489, 2620, 2674, 2751,
2896, 2917, 2983, 2990, 2995,
3000, 3016, 3025, 3026, 3033,
3034, 3035, 3037, 3041, 3056,
3057, 3063, 3065, 3090, 3107,
3179, 3236, 3325, 3634, 3646,
3648, 3726, 3801, 3904, 3913,
3926, 4350, 4360(a), 4401,
4429, 4454, 4511, 4520, 4537,
7918, 8780, 8782, 11007, 11201-
3, 11939, 13230-36, 13643,
13788, 13791-93, 13795, 14114,
14139, 14146-47, 14150-51,
14437, 14441-42, 14467, 14566,
14837-38, 15066, 15444, 16489,
16490, 16702, 16810, 16882,
17070, 17121, 17127, 18093-94,
18198

Smith, Mrs. Gladys, 1752, 13989

Sodinda, Muriel, 3220-21, 9966

Solanky, Dr., 9581, 9589, 9599

Susser, M., 1582

Szur, Dr., 1858, 2375, 2486, 8698,
8701

Tamara, Dora, 1796, 2137, 2506

Tambo, Oliver, 235, 276, 343, 404,
614, 761, 787, 790, 793, 820,
883, 884, 927, 1436, 1780, 2042,
2068, 2145, 2211-12, 2356, 2422,
3117, 3156, 3164-65, 3178, 3217,
3222, 3368, 3410-12, 3419-20,
3423, 3425, 3428-32, 3554, 3564,
3779, 3783, 3788, 3789, 3791,
3812, 3813, 3834, 4021, 4062,
4173, 4308, 4326, 4329, 4337,
4343, 4344, 4352, 4383, 4457,
4480, 4491, 4495, 4601, 8351,
8404, 8519, 8696, 8956, 8988,
9242, 10903, 10912, 11242,
11252, 11813, 11818, 11822-24,
11825, 11907-10, 11914, 13014,
13020, 13022-24, 13575, 13882,
13903-4, 14412-13, 15067, 15414,
15760, 15776, 15820, 16181,
16203, 16414, 16438, 16804,
16808, 17170, 17172, 17303,
17304, 17488, 17500, 17502,
17511, 17513, 17740, 17808

Tefu, S., 4326, 4327

Thaele, Mrs., 15269

Thandray, N., 1125, 1855, 1927,
8328, 8330, 15049, 15130

Thompson, Rev. Douglas C., 510,
744, 830, 914, 921, 1620, 1706,
1707, 1853-54, 1855, 1895, 1898,
1900-1901, 1911, 1916, 1920,
1928, 1932, 2062, 2064, 2072,
2211, 2227, 2247-48, 2249, 2347,

Thompson, Rev. Douglas C. (continued)
2394, 2397, 2414, 2418, 2487, 2627, 2715-16, 2726, 2733, 2735, 2739, 2745-46, 2751, 2795, 2840, 3090, 3197, 3203, 3204, 3337, 3890-93, 3955, 4054, 4099, 4101, 4518, 4580, 7600, 7607, 7609, 7620, 7623, 7631-33, 7653, 7851, 7932, 7937, 7957, 7966, 8278, 8329, 8332, 8334, 8337, 8391, 8452, 8487-89, 8491-92, 8556, 8703, 9453, 9970, 11006, 12007, 14114, 14438, 14838, 14848, 15213, 15438, 15459-60, 16029-30, 16034

Thorne, Athol, 1528, 1568, 2085, 2086, 3233

Tloome, D., 404, 961, 993, 1855, 1911, 1916, 2890, 2892, 2908, 2952, 3324, 3415, 3510, 3575, 3810, 3828, 4074, 4438, 8988, 9675, 9770, 10086, 11813, 14839, 15248, 15722, 15828, 16065, 16882, 17075, 17121, 17175, 17176, 17177, 18197, 18212

Tsehlane, Andrew, 16803

Tsekeletsa, Rev. A.A., 18276

Tsele, Peter, 3413, 10057

Tsele, Stephen, 16802, 16966

Tshabalala, Henry, 4127, 4138, 8192, 8940, 8944, 8951, 8953, 8957, 8961, 8979, 8991, 9174, 9226, 9293-94, 9300, 9308, 9321, 9789, 16991, 17120, 17160

Tshume, G.X., 16351, 16352

Tshume, T., 223, 325, 326, 339, 2445, 2478, 2772, 3166, 3810, 3811, 3812, 3815, 3821, 3822, 3823, 3824, 3825, 3828, 3833, 3850, 3984, 3997, 4256, 4257, 4258, 4267, 4270, 9489, 9491, 9540, 9542, 9551, 9557, 9626, 9641, 9648-49, 9652, 9668-71, 9676, 9681, 9688, 9693, 9698, 9709-10, 9723, 9728, 9739, 9741, 9755-56, 9768-70, 9811, 9994, 11047, 11078, 11910, 14394, 15624, 15630, 15639, 15685, 15707, 15744, 15745, 16259, 16368, 18036-38, 18092

Tshume, Rev. W.B., 4599, 18276

Tshunungwa, T.E., 217-18, 223, 273, 345, 361-62, 942, 1197, 1375, 1449, 1492, 1581, 1584, 2282, 2284, 2343, 2445, 2683, 2774, 2885, 3418, 3427, 3430-31, 3661-63, 3672-73, 3774, 3780, 3783, 3785, 3786, 3787, 3788, 3789, 3790, 3791, 3793, 3795, 3796, 3798, 3801, 3845, 4008, 4018, 4021-22, 4140, 4144, 4165, 4206, 4274, 4327, 4333, 4367, 4475, 9246, 9480, 9511, 9515, 9519, 9551-52, 9729-31, 9881-82, 9884-87, 9919, 9986, 10002-3, 10006, 10008, 10911, 10943, 10951, 10977, 11154, 11231, 11813, 11814, 11818, 11828, 11831, 11911-12, 13483, 13788, 15624-26, 15702, 15745, 16160, 16199-16200, 16256, 16968-69, 16982, 17904-5, 17975-76, 18038-39, 18102-3, 18162, 18163, 18192, 18199, 18236, 18308

Tunzi, Robertson, 3095, 3165, 8364, 8932, 8939-40, 8942, 8957, 8969, 8973, 8976, 9152, 9169, 9172, 9234, 9298, 9338, 10096, 13536

Turok, Ben, 404, 789, 942, 1051, 1375, 1581, 1582, 1591, 1642, 1665, 2072, 2084, 2726, 3801, 4139, 4499, 4558, 4563-64, 4569, 9018, 9022, 9028, 9033, 9043, 9067-68, 9071, 9081, 14428-29, 14440, 14445

Twaku, Ben, 3784, 3785, 3794

Twala, Mrs., 2856, 17513

INDEXES

Tyiki, Simon, 499, 503, 1334, 1492, 2143, 3165, 4393, 4454, 8364, 8509-10, 8518, 8927, 8930, 8936-37, 8939-40, 8943, 8946, 8953, 8958, 8960, 8973, 9147-50, 9174, 9179, 9229-31, 9234, 9293, 9300, 9305, 9307, 9322, 9577, 9586, 9856, 10096-97, 10099, 11231, 14864, 16157, 16821, 16991

Van der Ross, Dr. Richard E., 689, 15260-61, 15264-66

Vundla, P.Q., 345, 352, 361-62, 2708, 3120, 3122, 3557, 3788, 3789, 3798, 7412, 7420, 7424-26, 7428, 7485, 7487, 7946, 8358, 8360, 8364, 8366-67, 8427, 8432, 8517, 8969, 8992, 9168, 9238, 9309-10, 9332, 9856, 10087, 10092, 10951, 10975, 10976, 11247, 11261, 11339, 11813, 11822-24, 11826-27, 11831, 11977, 11978, 13589, 14412, 14657-58, 14681, 15300, 15301, 15413-14, 16172, 16438, 16808, 17162, 17387, 17432

Watts, Hilda (Mrs. Lionel Bernstein), 309, 1780, 1807, 1828, 1851-53, 1855, 1862, 1898, 1911-12, 1914, 1918, 1920, 1942, 2137, 2345, 2347, 2356, 2471, 2890, 2952, 2983, 2999, 3000, 3024, 3026, 3034, 3592, 4220, 7918, 8325-26, 8334-35, 8337, 8352, 8426, 9135, 9873, 13989, 14200, 14441, 14839, 14848, 15066, 16022

Weinberg, Eli, 204, 1865, 3098, 7406-7, 7918, 8350-51, 8404-5, 8425, 8518

Weinberg, Mrs. V., 1582, 1635, 8357, 14876, 15560

Williams, Cecil, 1780, 2090, 2254

Williams, Sophie, 4097, 8274, 14726-27, 15367-68, 15527

Wolfson, I., 3197

Wolpe, Harold, 2346, 7435, 8687

Xuma, Dr. A.B., 802, 997, 998, 2775, 4204, 8433, 8854, 9242, 9892, 10089, 10867, 10963, 13904, 14981-83, 15077, 16405, 17564-66, 17879-80, 17882, 17887, 17899-17900, 17934, 17969-70, 18205, 18206, 18207, 18216, 18245, 18246

Yengwa, M.B., 225, 277, 295, 326, 404, 985, 2077, 2078, 2079, 2810, 3222, 3423, 3663, 3668, 3672, 3702, 3709, 3714, 3724, 3790, 3791, 3792, 4161, 4167, 4170, 4182, 4193, 4197-4200, 4210-11, 4213, 4245, 4572, 4576, 4611, 8027, 8815, 9976, 10951, 10953, 10954, 10955, 10957, 11172, 11296, 11316, 11813, 11877, 13274

BIBLIOGRAPHY

Books and Pamphlets

Benson, Mary. THE AFRICAN PATRIOTS: THE STORY OF THE AFRICAN NATIONAL CONGRESS OF SOUTH AFRICA. London, Faber and Faber, [1963]. 310 p.

Brookes, Edgar H., and Macaulay, J.B. CIVIL LIBERTY IN SOUTH AFRICA. Cape Town, Oxford University Press, [1958]. 175 p.

Callan, Edward. ALBERT JOHN LUTHULI AND THE SOUTH AFRICAN RACE CONFLICT. Kalamazoo, Western Michigan University Press, [1962]. 75 p.

Feit, Edward. SOUTH AFRICA: THE DYNAMICS OF THE AFRICAN NATIONAL CONGRESS. London, Oxford University Press, [1962]. 73 p.

Forman, Lionel, and Sachs, E.S. THE SOUTH AFRICAN TREASON TRIAL. London, John Calder, [1957]. 216 p. New York, Monthly Review Press, [1958]. 216 p.

Hutchinson, Alfred. ROAD TO GHANA. London, Victor Gollancz, [1960]. 190 p.

International Commission of Jurists (founded 1952). SOUTH AFRICA AND THE RULE OF LAW. Geneva, [1960]. 239 p.

Joseph, Helen. IF THIS BE TREASON. London, Andre Deutsch, [1963]. 192 p.

Kuper, Leo. PASSIVE RESISTANCE IN SOUTH AFRICA. London, Cape, [1956]. 256 p. New Haven, Yale University Press, [1957]. 256 p.

Luthuli, Albert John. LET MY PEOPLE GO: AN AUTOBIOGRAPHY. Johannesburg, Collins, [1962]. 256 p. New York, McGraw-Hill, [1962]. 255 p.

Reeves, Ambrose. SOUTH AFRICA--YESTERDAY AND TOMORROW: A CHALLENGE TO CHRISTIANS. London, Victor Gollancz, [1962]. 173 p.

Sampson, Anthony. THE TREASON CAGE: THE OPPOSITION ON TRIAL IN SOUTH AFRICA. London, Heinemann, [1958]. 242 p.

Segal, Ronald. POLITICAL AFRICA: A WHO'S WHO OF PERSONALITIES AND PARTIES. London, Stevens and Sons, [1961]. New York, Frederick A. Praeger [1961]. 475 p.

SOUTH AFRICA'S TREASON TRIAL. [Johannesburg, "Afrika!" Publications, 1957. 24 p. Includes a photograph of each of the 156 who were arrested.

BIBLIOGRAPHY

Selected Articles

Two publications were issued regularly in mimeographed form by the Treason Trial [sometimes "Trials"] Defence Fund in Johannesburg: Press Summary, Nos. 1 through 58, Aug. 9, 1958, through March 29, 1961, and Treason Trial Bulletin, Nos. 1 through 13, [Feb. ?] 1958 through May 1961.

The periodicals Africa South, Drum, and Economist also contain material and commentary on the treason trial. See those entries below (in which the articles are arranged chronologically).

Africa South. Saunderson, Gordon. "JOHANNESBURG DIARY." 1, No. 3 (April-June 1957): 17-20.
    Junod, Violaine. "THE WHITE LIBERALS AND THE TREASON ARRESTS." 1, No. 3 (April-June 1957): 21-27.
    O'Dowd, Tony. "THE TRIAL TAKES SHAPE." 2, No. 1 (Oct.-Dec. 1957): 51-53.
    ————. "THE TRIAL TAKES SHAPE (II)." 2, No. 2 (Jan.-March 1958): 34-36.
    Bloom, Harry. "THE TRIAL TAKES SHAPE (III)." 2, No. 4 (July-Sept. 1958): 51-57.
    Leonard, D.A. "THE TRIAL BEGINS." 3, No. 2 (Jan.-March 1959): 39-47.
    Troup, Freda. "THE TREASON TRIAL--FOREVER?" 4, No. 1 (Oct.-Dec. 1959): 57-63.
    ————. "FOUR YEARS OF TREASON." 5, No. 2 (Jan.-March 1961): 56-62.
    ————. "THE HEIGHT OF TREASON." 5, No. 4 (July-Sept. 1961): 13-16.

Bentwich, Norman. "APARTHEID, THE SOUTH AFRICAN TREASON TRIAL AND HUMAN RIGHTS," Contemporary Review, 199 (Feb. 1961): 76-79.

Blom-Cooper, L.J. "THE SOUTH AFRICAN TREASON TRIAL: R. v. ADAMS AND OTHERS," International and Comparative Law Quarterly, 8 (Jan. 1959): 59-72.

Brockway, Fenner. "THE SOUTH AFRICAN TREASON TRIAL," Monthly Review, 9 (March 1958): 392-394.

Drum. "TREASON ARRESTS!" Jan. 1957, pp. 17-19.
    "BIG NOISY TRIAL!" Feb. 1957, pp. 19-27.
    "TREASON: END OF ROUND ONE!" Sept. 1957, pp. 18-27.
    "TREASON TRIAL DEFENDANTS." Aug. 1958, pp. 26-29.
    "THE CROWN VERSUS 91." Sept. 1958, pp. 19-21.
    "TREASON TRIAL HALTS." Nov. 1958, pp. 80-81.

Economist. "SOUTH AFRICAN POLITICAL TRIALS." 181 (Dec. 15, 1956): 955-956.
    "SOUTH AFRICA'S REICHSTAG FIRE TRIALS." 182 (Jan. 12, 1957): 121-122.
    "THE SOUTH AFRICAN TREASON TRIALS." 182 (March 2, 1957): 716.
    "WITHOUT REDRESS." 185 (Dec. 21, 1957): 1040.
    "MEASURE FOR MEASURE." 186 (Feb. 8, 1958): 474.
    "THE WIG TOPPLES." 188 (July 19, 1958): 192.

Economist (continued).

        LETTER by A.W. Steward. 188 (July 26, 1958): 284.
        "THE LAW'S DELAY." 189 (Oct. 18, 1958): 216.
        "TREASON ON ITS LAST LEGS." 192 (Aug. 15, 1959): 408.
        "TURBULENT JUDGE." 199 (April 8, 1961): 113-114.

Fairbairn, James. "THE BAASKAP TRIAL," New Statesman, 56 (Aug. 2, 1958): 133.

———. "THE EXPERT WITNESS," ibid., 58 (Nov. 28, 1959): 735-736.

———. "FREEDOM IN THEIR LIFETIME," ibid., 57 (Jan. 17, 1959): 60-61.

———. "NO FLYING SQUADS," ibid., 55 (Feb. 8, 1958): 160.

Gardiner, Gerald. "THE SOUTH AFRICAN TREASON TRIAL," Journal of the International Commission of Jurists, 1 (Autumn 1957): 43-58.

Griswold, Erwin N. "TREASON TRIAL IN SOUTH AFRICA," The Times (London), Sept. 25, 1958, p. 11.

Houser, George M. "TREASON IN SOUTH AFRICA?" Christian Century, 74 (March 6, 1957): 288-289.

Huddleston, Trevor. "THE TREASON TRIAL," New Statesman, 52 (Dec. 15, 1956): 780.

Karis, Thomas G. "THE SOUTH AFRICAN TREASON TRIAL," Political Science Quarterly, 76 (June 1961): 217-240.

Lewin, Julius. "BEHIND THE TREASON TRIAL IN SOUTH AFRICA," Monthly Review, 10 (Oct. 1958): 210-216.

Mackenzie, Kenneth. "GUILTY MEN," Spectator, 206 (April 7, 1961), 464-465.

"THE NATS AGAIN THWARTED," New Statesman, 57 (April 25, 1959): 562.

Paton, Alan. "ON TRIAL FOR TREASON," New Republic, 137 (Nov. 11, 1957): 9-12.

———. "SOUTH AFRICAN TREASON TRIAL," Atlantic, 205 (Jan. 1960): 78-81.

"THE RED AND THE BLACK," New Statesman, 61 (April 7, 1961): 534-535.

Sampson, Anthony. "TREASON IN BLACK AND WHITE," Nation, 187 (Aug. 16, 1958): 72-73.

"THE SOUTH AFRICAN TREASON TRIAL," Bulletin of the International Commission of Jurists, No. 9 (Aug. 1959), pp. 21-26.

"THE SOUTH AFRICAN TREASON TRIAL: SECOND PHASE," ibid., No. 8 (Dec. 1958), pp. 45-53.

"TREASON IN SOUTH AFRICA," New Republic, 139 (Dec. 8, 1958): 6.